The 11ᵗʰ Commandment

MORE INSIGHTS INTO THE ONE
ANOTHERS OF SCRIPTURE

Volume 2

Don McMinn

©6Acts Press
2322 Creekside Circle South
Irving, TX 75063
972.432.8690
djmcminn@msn.com
www.6Acts.org

D1122207

The 11th Commandment—Volume 2

More Insights Into the One Anothers of Scripture

Don McMinn

First edition—2002
2322 Creekside Circle South, Irving, Texas, 75063
972.432.8690

Printed in the United States for Worldwide Distribution
ISBN—0-9703229-3-3

Contents

DEDICATION

In a magazine cartoon, a thief was wearing a "Lone Ranger" mask. His gun was pointed at his frightened victim as he yelled: "Okay, gimme all your valuables!" The victim began stuffing into the sack all his friends.

My most precious "possessions" are my friends and family. This workbook is lovingly dedicated to these friends who helped inspire the message of this project. To these friends I am devoted:

Lee and Linda Blackwell
Dean and Nawanda Fuller
Tom and Kay Hill
David and Lisa Holmes
Bobby and Liz Kimberlin
Gene and Donna Lucas
Ron and Liane Nicol
Phil and Vicki Northen
Dean and Andrea Satchwell
Mike and Marcy Zarlengo

My deepest appreciation goes to David Ferguson and Intimate Life Ministries, a leader in the area of Great Commandment Ministry. I served on their staff for five years, during which time I learned the importance of, and the basis of, relational ministry. They offer excellent training and resources in the area of loving God and others. I encourage you to visit their web site for more information.
www.GreatCommandment.net

INTRODUCTION

Imagine the stir that Jesus must have caused when, during his final conversation with his disciples, he announced a new commandment, essentially the 11th Commandment. This new commandment, recorded in John 13:34, challenged the disciples with a new paradigm. His statement was significant and strategic.

One phrase at a time, his command says:

- "Love one another."
- "As I have loved you, so you must love one another."
- "All men will know that you are my disciples if you love one another."

But while the disciples no doubt must have sensed the gravity of Jesus' statement, they also might have been a bit frustrated. Love is, after all, a big concept that defies simple definition. The challenge is, when God says, "Love one another," what are we to *do? How* are we to love one another?

The hypothesis of this book is that - the mysterious "how-to" of love is practically explained by the One Anothers of Scripture.

Thirty-five times in the New Testament, we see a recurring word pattern—an action verb followed by the words *"one another."* We are told to: prefer, accept, greet, encourage, forgive, comfort, wait for, and honor...one another. These verbs, when substituted for the word *"love"* in John 13:34, teach us the "how-to" of love.

The 11th Commandment Workbook, volume 1, covered eight of the One Anothers:

- Encourage
- Prefer
- Accept

- Greet
- Comfort
- Carry Burdens

- Forgive
- Admonish

This workbook, *The 11th Commandment*, volume 2, will cover eleven more:

- Pray for
- Wait for
- Honor
- Offer Hospitality to

- Live in Peace with
- Care for
- Confess Your Faults to
- Be Devoted to

- Serve
- Be Kind to
- Spur on toward Love and Good Deeds

The 11th Commandment workbooks remove the ambiguity from the command to love others. They will guide you to a new understanding of what it means to love others as God has loved you.

Completing the first workbook is not a prerequisite for understanding and benefiting from the sequel. Each chapter of both books "stands alone." The lessons are not progressive or cumulative. If you have not read the first workbook, it would, however, be advantageous to read at least chapter one because it presents some foundational principles that apply to all of the One Anothers. Chapter one of the first workbook can be read or downloaded, free of charge, from the 6Acts web site—www.6Acts.org. At the bottom of the home page, click on the *11th Commandment* icon and then click on the icon that reads *Click Here for Chapter One*. All 11th Commandment resources can also be ordered on the web site (see the *Resources* icon).

Each chapter of this workbook includes fill-in-the-blank sections and a Personal Journal section. Though it takes time to thoughtfully answer these questions, your understanding of the material will be greatly enhanced by doing so.

You can benefit from the material by completing the workbook on your own, but it is best to work through the material with a group or at least another individual. The Group Discussion Questions at the end of each chapter suggest thought-provoking issues that will take you deeper into each topic.

Our prayer is that God will use these workbooks to teach us how to *love one another*, because, according to the apostle Paul, love is the supreme issue in the kingdom of God:

- Love is greater than faith and hope (1 Corinthians 13:13).
- All other commandments are summed up in the one command: "Love your neighbor as yourself" (Romans 13:9).
- Without love, acts of ministry are meaningless (1 Corinthians 13:1–3).
- Love is the fulfillment of the law (Romans 13:10).

God has challenged me with this directive: *Learn how to minister all thirty-five of the One Anothers and then spend the rest of your life loving others in these practical ways.* This is, after all, the second part of the Great Commandment (Matthew 22:39). It is the essence of the Christian life.

General William Booth was the founder of the Salvation Army. One year he was scheduled to be the keynote speaker at their annual meeting but became ill and was not able to attend. He cabled the delegates a message that contained one word: "Others!"

Indeed, the "delivery system" of the gospel message always involves ministering to others. It's not about me; it's about others.

But if I'm always focusing on others, what should I do about my needs? Lucy, in the popular comic strip "Peanuts," had the same question. She asks Charlie Brown, "Why are we here on earth?" He answers, "To make others happy." She thinks about that for a while and then asks, "Then why are the others here?"

Good question. And the answer is, "To make you happy."

From my perspective, I am to focus on others; from their perspective, they should focus on me. When everyone does his part, everyone's needs are met. It's the reciprocal aspect of the One Anothers, a constant giving and receiving of God's gracious gifts.

Ministering to others will bring a deepened sense of meaning and joy to our lives for Jesus taught that, "it is more blessed to give than to receive" (Acts 20:35). Minister the One Anothers and you will sense the favor of God upon your life.

The One Anothers

1. Love one another (John 13:34).
2. Depend on one another (Romans 12:5 AMP).
3. Be devoted to one another (Romans 12:10).
4. Wash each other's feet (John 13:14).
5. Rejoice with one another (Romans 12:15; 1 Corinthians 12:26).
6. Weep with one another (Romans 12:15).
7. Live in harmony with one another (Romans 12:16).
8. Don't judge one another (Romans 14:13).
9. Accept one another (Romans 15:7).
10. Admonish one another (Colossians 3:16).
11. Greet one another (Romans 16:16).
12. Wait for one another (1 Corinthians 11:33).
13. Care for one another (1 Corinthians 12:25).
14. Serve one another (Galatians 5:13).
15. Be kind to one another (Ephesians 4:32).
16. Forgive one another (Ephesians 4:32; Colossians 3:13).
17. Be compassionate toward one another (Ephesians 4:32).
18. Encourage one another (1 Thessalonians 5:11).
19. Submit to one another (Ephesians 5:21).
20. Bear with one another (Ephesians 4:2; Colossians 3:13).
21. Spur one another on to love and good deeds (Hebrews 10:24).
22. Offer hospitality to one another (1 Peter 4:9).
23. Minister gifts to one another (1 Peter 4:10).
24. Be clothed in humility toward one another (1 Peter 5:5).
25. Don't slander one another (James 4:11).
26. Don't grumble against one another (James 5:9).
27. Confess your sins to one another (James 5:16).
28. Pray for one another (James 5:16).
29. Fellowship with one another (1 John 1:7).
30. Don't be puffed up against one another (1 Corinthians 4:6).
31. Carry one another's burdens (Galatians 6:2).
32. Honor one another (Romans 12:10).
33. Instruct one another (Romans 15:14).
34. Prefer one another (Romans 12:10).
35. Comfort one another (2 Corinthians 1:4).

PRAY FOR ONE ANOTHER
"Pray for each another" (James 5:16).

One Sunday night in April 1912, a weary American woman could not sleep because her spirit was troubled. She felt burdened to pray, so she earnestly began to pray for her husband, who was then in the mid-Atlantic, homeward bound on the *Titanic*. As the hours went by she could get no assurance, so she continued praying until about five o'clock in the morning, when she felt a great peace and drifted off to sleep.

Meanwhile her husband, Colonel Gracie, was among the hundreds of people who were frantically trying to launch the lifeboats from the great ship that had been pierced by an iceberg. Gracie had given up all hope of being saved and was doing his best to help the women and children. Wishing that he could get a last message through to his wife, he cried from his heart, "Good-bye, my darling!" As the ship plunged to her watery grave, Gracie was sucked down in the giant whirlpool. Instinctively he began to swim under the ice-cold water, barely clinging to life.

Suddenly he came to the surface and found himself near an overturned lifeboat. Along with several others, he climbed aboard and was picked up by another lifeboat about five o'clock in the morning, at the very time that peace came to his praying wife.

This is a rather dramatic example of the value of praying for others. Personally, I've never had such a spectacular answer to prayer (though I probably have; I'm just not aware of it). But I can recall hundreds of times when Pray for One Another was just the right expression of God's grace. For example:

- I prayed for many years for the woman who would become my wife, and God gave me Mary.
- I prayed that my daughter would get accepted into just the right college, and she did.
- I prayed that my friend would survive surgery, and he's alive and well.
- I prayed that my co-worker would be delivered from depression, and she was.

- I prayed that my friend's daughter would live, and she didn't. But I'm still glad I prayed.

In this short chapter, I don't feel compelled, nor do I have the space or expertise to comment on the theology of prayer. Quite frankly, I'm not sure that we need to be convinced of the efficacy of prayer, nor do we need instruction on how to pray. We just need to do it.

Write about a time when God answered your prayers concerning another individual.

_____

_____

As with all the other One Anothers, Christ is not asking us to do something that he has not and is not doing for us. The apostle Paul assured us that Christ is "at the right hand of God and is also interceding for us" (Romans 8:34). This blessed thought caused Robert McCheyne to say, "If I could hear Christ praying for me in the next room, I would not fear a million enemies. Yet distance makes no difference. He is praying for me."

Different Types of Prayer

The apostle Paul makes it clear that there are different types of prayers: "And pray in the Spirit on all occasions *with all kinds of prayer*" (Ephesians 6:18; emphasis added). The types of prayer include:

- **Prayers of confession**—"God, have mercy on me, a sinner" (Luke 18:13).
- **Prayers of gratitude**—"I always thank God for you" (1 Corinthians 1:4).
- **Prayers of worship**—"I thank and praise you, O God" (Daniel 2:23).
- **Personal prayers**—"Oh, that you would bless me and enlarge my territory" (1 Chronicles 4:10).

The admonition to Pray for One Another is **intercessory prayer**. Intercession is making an appeal or petition on behalf of someone else. Christ is involved in this ministry: "He [Jesus] always lives to intercede for them" (Hebrews 7:25), as is the Holy Spirit, "The Spirit himself intercedes for us with groans that words cannot express" (Romans 8:26).

Prerequisites for Praying for One Another

1. In your relationships, develop a deep level of care, vulnerability, and trust so that people will feel safe in sharing personal prayer requests with you.

I can usually assess how emotionally close a group of people is by simply asking for prayer requests. For instance, I recently taught a weekend retreat for a church and we ended the Friday evening session with a time of prayer. When I asked, "Does anyone have a prayer request?" I received these responses:

- *Please pray for one of my co-workers. Her daughter was diagnosed with cancer.*
- *I have an aunt who lives in Chicago. The pastor of her church abruptly resigned and it has thrown the church into chaos.*
- *We need to pray for our elected officials in Washington, D.C.*

Interestingly, not one prayer request was for anyone in the room—they all involved "long-distance" needs. While there's certainly nothing wrong with voicing these types of prayer concerns, it doesn't satisfy the admonition to Pray for One Another. We need to pray *for one another*. The emphasis should be on, "How can I pray for *you?*" – not, your co-worker's daughter, your aunt's church, or our nation's elected officials.

In other groups, vulnerable sharing goes a little deeper. When asked, "How can I pray for you?" the responses might include:

- *We're going on vacation next week; pray that we'll have a safe trip.*
- *I'm trying to sell my car; pray that it will sell.*
- *Pray for my father. He fell and broke his leg.*

Again, there's nothing wrong with these requests and they should certainly be prayed for, but we need to go deeper still. Imagine the closeness and security of a friendship in which these types of requests could be voiced:

- *We're really struggling with my son. He's starting to have a rebellious attitude, and we don't know how to handle it.*
- *I've been feeling depressed lately.*
- *I'm really unhappy at my job.*

Hopefully, in time, our prayer requests can include personal, deeply felt needs.

One of the best ways to encourage others to be vulnerable about their needs is to be open about your own. Vulnerability must be reciprocal. I shouldn't expect you to share your struggles with me, unless I am willing to share mine with you. We must also develop a genuine sense of care for others. Why would someone be willing to be vulnerable and share her prayer requests with me if she's not convinced that I am concerned for and interested in her life?

> Pray for One Another will become natural and effective when our relationships are a "safe place."

Pray for One Another will become natural and effective when our relationships are a "safe place." Likewise, our churches, small groups—any corporate expression of the body of Christ—must have this "safe" dimension.

Do you have a friend or friends with whom you can share your deepest needs? Do you feel comfortable being vulnerable about your needs (prayer requests) with them? Explain.

_____

_____

2. Establish a secure measure of confidentiality in your friendships.

Whenever I counsel people, at the beginning of the first session, I always reassure them of three things:

1. *There's nothing you can share with me that will cause me to love you less. What we talk about in our counseling sessions will not affect our friendship in any way.*

2. *There's nothing you can share with me that I haven't heard many times before. (People often think, I doubt if Pastor Don has ever heard anything as bad as this...)*

3. *I pledge to you complete confidentiality. Whatever you share with me will not be repeated to anyone else.*

For Pray for One Another to really work, these three assurances need to be in place. People will not be vulnerable with their needs and hurts unless they know that you will not think less of them because of their neediness and, that they are secure in your confidentiality.

Evaluate yourself relative to your ability to maintain confidentiality.

Practical Ways to Pray for One Another

1. Keep a prayer journal.

"I have written both of them as reminders" (2 Peter 3:1).

It helps to keep a written record of prayer needs and corresponding answers to prayer. Find a method that works for you. A prayer journal may be a single sheet of paper you keep in your Bible or in your daily planner. It may be a designated book. You may prefer to keep your prayer journal on your computer. Whatever system you adopt, use it regularly and keep it updated. I usually have several columns for continued prayer needs (for example, I pray for my family daily). I also maintain a column for temporary prayer requests (for instance, someone who is going to the doctor for tests).

2. Pray for people "on the spot."

"And when he had said this, he knelt down with all of them and prayed" (Act 20:36).

Whenever someone shares a prayer need with me or I sense she needs prayer, I ask to pray with her at that moment. I also assure her that I will continue to pray for her need in the future, but she will be uniquely blessed by being prayed for "on the spot." In this sense, consider changing the preposition in Pray *for* One Another to Pray *with* One Another. Many times we tell people, "I'll be praying for you," but then we inadvertently forget. Instead of making a promise I may forget to fulfill, I usually ask, "May I pray for you right now?" I have never been refused.

Also, don't hesitate to pray for someone over the telephone. It may seem awkward at first, but it is effective. I've even prayed for people through an e-mail message. Just type in a prayer and hit "send." The recipient will be blessed and, of course, God will hear as well.

Additionally, a major aspect of the ministry of Pray for One Another is the emotional/psychological blessing that comes from someone placing his hand on your shoulder and hearing him call out your name and your need to the Lord. This dimension is lost if we simply say, "I'll be praying for you" and fail to pray *with* a person.

3. Encourage people to share their needs and prayer requests.

"Brothers, pray for us" (1 Thessalonians 5:25).

In order for Pray for One Another to work best, we all need to share prayer requests. Though it is possible to discern the needs of others and pray for them even if they don't request prayer, it's beneficial and even therapeutic for all of us to voice our requests. Sharing prayer requests with others requires humility on our part and underscores the interdependence of the body of Christ. When we share prayer requests, we confess our neediness of God and others. If a person never expresses any prayer needs, he may suffer from self-reliance and self-sufficiency.

Many times we tell people, *"I'll be praying for you,"* but then we inadvertently forget. Instead of making a promise **I may forget to fulfill**, I usually ask, "May I pray for you right now?" *I have never been refused.*

4. Let people know that you are praying for them.

"We constantly pray for you" (2 Thessalonians 1:11).

When you pray for people, tell them. They will be blessed to know that you were thinking of them and that you care for them. Your prayers may also encourage them to seek God themselves.

5. Whenever possible, pray for others about specific areas of concern.

"I pray that you may be active in sharing your faith" (Philemon 1:6).

While it is okay to pray a general prayer for someone, such as, "Lord, bless John," it is more effective to pray specifically, "Lord, help John find a job." We often pray only in generalities, like the ten-year-old boy who put his prayer request in the offering plate—*Dear Pastor, please pray for all the airline pilots. I am flying to California tomorrow.*

6. Designate a specific time and place to pray for others.

"Jesus went out into the hills to pray, and spent the night praying to God" (Luke 6:12).

[Also see Matthew 14:23, Mark 6:46, and Luke 9:28. Apparently, Jesus often went into the hills to pray.]

It's best to have a consistent, predetermined time and place to pray. I pray every morning for my family and friends while sitting in my den. I often set aside one day a month for a time of prayer and fasting.

7. Maintain spontaneous times of prayer.

"We constantly pray for you" (2 Thessalonians 1:11).

While it's helpful to maintain a daily ritual of prayer (see #6 above), it's also good to "pray continually" (1 Thessalonians 5:17). During the day—while driving around town or eating lunch—pray for others. When someone "pops into your mind," accept that as a cue from God to pray for that person.

8. Realize that praying for others will be demanding on us.

"He [Epaphras] is always wrestling in prayer for you" (Colossians 4:12).

As with all of the One Anothers, Pray for One Another is a service that requires time and effort, especially when the burdens of others become our own burden (2 Corinthians 11:28).

J. Oswald Sanders offers valuable insight on this idea of wrestling in prayer for others:

> The word "wrestling" (in Colossians 4:12) is that from which our word "agony" is derived. It is used of a man toiling at his work until utterly weary (Colossians 1:29), or competing in the arena for the coveted laurel wreath (1 Corinthians 9:25). It describes the soldier battling for his life (1 Timothy 6:12), or a man struggling to deliver his friend from danger (John 18:36). It pictures the agony of earnestness of a man to save his own soul (Luke 13:24). But its supreme significance appears in the tragedy of Gethsemane. "Being in an agony he prayed more earnestly" (Luke 22:44), an agony induced by His identification with and grief over the sins of a lost world. Prayer is evidently a strenuous spiritual exercise, which demands the utmost mental discipline and concentration.

Write about a time when you "wrestled" in prayer for someone.

9. Pray continually for others.
"We have not stopped praying for you" (Colossians 1:9).

We will often be called upon to pray for someone for a long time, perhaps years. For example, one day George Muller, a nineteenth-century preacher known for establishing orphanages to care for thousands of English children, began praying for five of his friends. After many months, one of them came to the Lord. Ten years later, two others were converted. It took twenty-five years before the fourth man was saved. Muller persevered in prayer until his death for the fifth friend, and throughout those fifty-two years he never gave up hoping that he would accept Christ! His faith was rewarded, for soon after Muller's funeral, the last one was saved.

Are there any issues that you have been praying about for years?

10. See Pray for One Another as a cue to engage in other One Anothers.

As we pray for others we will become aware of other One Anothers that may need to be ministered. For instance, my wife and I invited several couples over for dinner one evening (Offer Hospitality to One Another), and after dinner we had a time of prayer. One couple, who were new to our church, shared that the husband had lost his job several months before. They were obviously struggling emotionally, financially, and spiritually. As a group, we immediately comforted them (Comfort One Another) and then prayed together. Our time together became a precursor for further ministry.

- *Encourage One Another*—I called them weekly to see how they were doing.
- *Bear One Another's Burdens*—I e-mailed his resume to our church leadership and made several calls to friends who could also help spread the word.
- *Honor One Another*—I discovered that the wife enjoyed singing and the husband was a gifted teacher, so I made some calls and got them involved in the choir and teaching a Bible study.

Final Thoughts

Before ending this chapter, I want to comment on some issues that often bother me when I hear people praying for others. These are personal "burrs under my saddle" [Or, as the apostle Paul would say, "I have no command from the Lord, but I give a judgment" (1 Corinthians 7:25)]. You may disagree with me, but it will be therapeutic for me to voice them.

1. When praying for others, talk to God; don't talk to the person you're praying for.

I think we often inadvertently combine Encourage One Another and Pray for One Another. We'll begin our prayer by addressing God, "Dear Father," but at some point in the prayer we'll start preaching to the person we're praying for, saying phrases like:

- *God, in your word you said that you would never leave us or forsake us, you're the ever-present one. You're with Mark right now in the midst of his troubles.* Does God really need to be reminded of this? Mark may indeed need to be reminded of this precious truth, but share it with him before you begin to pray (Encourage One Another).
- *God, I'm so sorry that Mark is hurting; He's been through a really tough time, and I know he feels overwhelmed.* These are wonderful words of comfort (Comfort One Another), but they would best be spoken to Mark before the prayer time begins.

When we pray for another person he will undoubtedly be blessed by "overhearing" our conversation with God, but refrain from carrying on a dual dialogue both with God and the person. Concentrate on speaking solely to God.

2. Avoid using trite, overused phrases.

Most of us who have grown up in the church have learned "prayer clichés" that we are tempted to use when praying. Phrases like: "Bless the hands of the physicians as they operate..." Likewise, avoid using what the Bible calls "vain repetitions," phrases that may indeed have a deep meaning but ones that are repeated so often that they have lost their meaning. When I was a boy, there was a man in our church who would pray the exact same prayer every week (I remember one phrase in particular, "Bless the gift and the giver"). Initially it was a beautiful, meaningful prayer but because it was repeated verbatim each week, it became meaningless.

> **When we** pray for another person he *will* undoubtedly *be blessed by* "over hearing" **our conversation with God,** but refrain from carrying on a dual dialogue both *with God and the person.*

3. Avoid using an "ecclesiastical voice" and seventeenth century English idioms.

Some people, when praying, adopt a totally different vocal sound. Their voice becomes deeper, more resonant, and louder. They have a "praying voice" and a "regular voice." This seems showy and ostentatious. Just use your normal tone of voice. You're praying to God, not to others, and God doesn't need to hear a different sonority when you're praying.

Likewise, avoid using "King James English"—phrases such as, "O God, Thou knowest all things, and by Thy divine sovereignty Thou hast ordained our days." They may have spoken that way back in 1611 when the King James Version of the Bible was written, but no one speaks like that today (even in England).

When done appropriately, praying for others can be a simple and short exercise, perhaps taking no longer than one to four minutes. We may erroneously think that the longer we pray for someone, the more effective our prayers ("A four-minute prayer is twice as effective as a two-minute one"), but that is not the case.

Also, when praying for someone, focus solely on the need that that person has at that particular moment. Avoid digressing into other areas of need (missionaries, the church, other people's needs, etc.).

Yogi Berra, the great baseball catcher, was playing in a ball game in which the score was tied, with two outs in the bottom of the ninth inning. The batter from the opposing team stepped up to the batting box and made the sign of the cross on home plate with his bat. Berra was a Catholic, too, but he wiped off the plate with his glove and said to the pious batter, "Why don't we let God just watch this game?"

That's good theology when applied to the outcome of a baseball game but terrible advice when it comes to the heartfelt needs of our friends. We need to intercede on behalf of our friends, asking for God's wisdom, mercy, and grace to be poured out on their lives. We need to continually approach the throne of God on behalf of our friends and ask God to exert himself strongly on their behalf.

We need to Pray for One Another.

Personal Journal

1. Of all the people you know, who is the most faithful to Pray for One Another?

_____

2. Who prays for you the most?

_____

3. If you were to keep a prayer journal, what would be the best system for you to use (see practical suggestion #1)?

_____

4. If you were to have a designated time and place to pray, when and where would it be (see practical suggestion #6)?

_____

5. Are you comfortable praying aloud? Are you comfortable praying for people "on the spot"? If not, why? Do you think you could ever feel comfortable praying aloud and spontaneously?

_____

_____

6. Write your own definition of Pray for One Another.

_____

_____

7. On a scale from 1 to 10 (1 being, "I need to improve" and 10 being, "I do a good job"), how well do you do at praying for others?

I rated myself a _____.

Group Time

Each member of the group should give his or her individual response to the first two questions. Allow about two minutes for each person's response. Allow all group members to share answers to question #1 before proceeding to question #2.

1. What was the most interesting concept in this chapter?
2. Share your responses to the first three Personal Journal questions.

As a group, process these discussion questions. The discussion questions have been prioritized. Depending on the time allotted for your group discussion, you may not be able to discuss all the questions.

a. Read Luke 11:5-13 and Luke 18:1-8 and discuss what these verses teach about prayer.
b. In Matthew 6:5-8, Jesus taught on prayer and warned against hypocrisy, incoherence, and long-windedness. How are we often guilty of these vices?
c. Read 1 Samuel 12:23 and discuss what the verse teaches about prayer.
d. Read the last phrase of James 5:16 and discuss what it teaches about prayer.
e. Read 2 Corinthians 1:10–11 and discuss what these verses teach about prayer.

WAIT FOR ONE ANOTHER

"Wait for each other" (1 Corinthians 11:33).

As I wrote this workbook, I continually asked the Lord to help me experience what I was writing. I wanted to understand each of the One Anothers in a deeper way than I had before. I vividly remember the day he taught me about Wait for One Another.

I had taken a small group of friends to see the sights and sounds of New York City for four days. There's a lot to see in the Big Apple, so each day's itinerary was well orchestrated and full. In New York City, walking is the preferred mode of transportation if you're traveling fewer than twenty blocks. So on the first day we walked from one place to the next, maintaining a quick pace as we went.

One member of our group, an older lady, had trouble keeping up the pace so she and her daughter walked together. The rest of our group would inevitably get several blocks ahead of them and then would have to stop and wait. I felt myself getting irritated at the constant delays, thinking, *This isn't fair. We have a lot to see and do, and one slow person should not set the pace of the entire group.*

The lady's daughter became exasperated at the pressure to keep the pace. She finally said, "Don, we just can't keep up. You're going too fast. Just go on without us." Immediately the Lord said to me, as clearly as if were displayed on a billboard in Times Square—*Wait for One Another.*

I accepted the Lord's rebuke, slowed down, and for the rest of the trip we adopted her pace. I actually enjoyed the trip more because I absorbed more at the slower pace and because there is joy in ministering the One Anothers, even waiting!

When we Wait for One Another, we abandon our own pace, agenda, abilities, strengths, and desires and yield to others. It is a practical and challenging manifestation of Prefer One Another.

Impatience

In our struggle to Wait for One Another, we will encounter an ugly vice called impatience. Impatience is a close relative of selfishness. We often become impatient when faced with irritations or opposition, but we are sorely tempted with impatience when faced with delay. We just don't want to slow down.

The opposite of impatience is, of course—patience. It is indeed a godly virtue.

> In our struggle to Wait for One Another, we will encounter an ugly vice called impatience.

- Ephesians 4:2 simply says, "Be patient."
- First Corinthians 13:4 uses the word to help define what love is, "Love is patient."
- Galatians 5:22 states that patience is a fruit of the Spirit; when he controls our lives, we will be patient.
- First Thessalonians 5:14 teaches that this grace gift is to be given to all, "Be patient with everyone." We can't pick and choose with whom we will be patient.

Bearing with the Weakness of Others

There is another One Another that is similar to, if not the same as, Wait for One Another. Ephesians 4:2 says, "Bear with one another in love." Romans 15:1-3 elaborates on the subject: "We who are strong ought to bear with the failings of the weak and not to please ourselves. For even Christ did not please himself."

These verses suggest that some members of the body of Christ are weaker than other parts. Paul plainly states this in 1 Corinthians 12:22-24 ,"On the contrary, those parts of the body that seem to be weaker are indispensable, and the parts that we think are less honorable we treat with special modesty, while our presentable parts need no special treatment."

When we who are strong, relate to those who are weak, we must *wait for* and *bear with* the weaker members.

But how are some members weaker?

There are indeed, several different dimensions to consider as we study the grace gift of Wait for One Another. We will be challenged to:

Wait for One Another *Physically*

Speed

We all function at different speeds. Some people are slow and deliberate, others are fast and decisive.

Sometimes the speed at which we operate is just a function of how God made us:

- One of my friends is a classic Type-A personality. He moves at the speed of light.
- Another friend moves in slow motion. He excels at what he does, but his pace is slow. He's a perfectionist plodder.

We may be slow in some areas and fast in others:
- My wife, Mary, can read a 420-page novel in about six hours; it takes me ten hours to read the same book.

- At a restaurant, I can decide what I want to order in ninety seconds; it takes Mary longer.

We all function at different speeds. Some people are slow and deliberate, others *are fast and decisive.*

Capacity

We all have different capacities, that is, the number of responsibilities/projects we are able to handle simultaneously. Picture several jugglers and consider their different capacities. One may be able to juggle only three objects, another can handle six, and a professional juggler may be able to negotiate ten.

Every person has his or her own capacity, a limit to how many projects that can be handled at one time.

- *Some people enjoy focusing on a few tasks.* My wife, Mary, is most comfortable focusing on a few things. When she's juggling three projects she's happy; pitch her a fourth responsibility and life gets too stressful. But she always does very well at what she does.
- *Some people can handle multiple tasks.* I can usually negotiate multiple projects at once. In any given period of time I'm usually working full-time at the church, writing a new book, landscaping the yard, helping a friend start a new ministry, hosting a minister's retreat, and coordinating an area-wide event…and I find the pace invigorating.
- *Some people can manage an incredible amount of projects.* I have a friend who can have twenty balls up in the air at the same time and not drop one.

Physical limits

We all have different physical limitations, depending on our:

- *Physical make-up*—Some people are simply more physically capable than others. Consider the advanced physical capacity and ability of a gifted athlete.
- *Age*—The older we get, the slower we become and the less agile we are.
- *Physical challenges*—Some people are limited by a physical handicap.
- *Sickness*—A temporary or prolonged physical illness can limit us.

Endurance

We all have different levels of endurance. Both physically and emotionally, some people get maxed-out more quickly than others. For instance, attending a three-day business conference may totally exhaust one employee but have no affect on another. One member of a travel group may feel overwhelmed after a day of sight-seeing while another member of the travel group may have lots of energy left.

In your relationships, in what ways are you often called upon to Wait for One Another relative to physical issues?

Wait for One Another *Emotionally*

Emotional struggles

Hurts—We may be called upon to Wait for people because their unhealed hurts cause them to be hesitant or slow.

- An individual who has been hurt deeply through divorce may be reticent to pursue another close relationship.
- A business partner may be overly conservative and cautious because of a painful bankruptcy in his former business. He's not willing to move as quickly as we want, so we need to slow down.

Fears—We should wait for others when they are fearful.

- A child may be afraid of the dark, so we may need to stay with her and postpone our going to bed.
- A loved one may be afraid of flying, making it necessary to plan on a driving trip.

Personality types

People who are more aggressive, extroverted, and adventurous may be called upon to wait for those who are shy, reticent, and cautious.

List several ways in which you are called upon to wait for other people in the area of emotions:

_____

_____

Wait for One Another *Mentally*

Different levels of intelligence

We each have a different IQ level. The ability to reason, memorize, learn, and perceive things logically differs with each person. This is just a fact of life. Often we will need to slow down in order to accommodate someone who is slower than we are mentally.

Also, we all have strengths and weaknesses in different subjects or areas. We may be very "bright" in one area but "slow" in another. For example, I've always had difficulty learning foreign languages. While other areas of study usually come easily, I've never been good at learning languages.

What areas of study have you typically struggled with (math, languages, etc.)?

_____

What areas of study are you good at? Because of your strength in these areas, these are the very areas you may be challenged to Wait for One Another.

_____

Different styles of communication

- Some people, when communicating verbally, take a long time to get to the point, while others are quick to reach the essence of a conversation.
- Some people talk in circles, often repeating themselves, while others are linear thinkers.
- Some people are so logical they cannot comprehend the emotional implications of a situation; while others are so emotional they cannot understand the logical implications.

Wait for One Another *Spiritually*

Different levels of spiritual zeal

We all experience different levels of spiritual zeal and passion. For instance, when I was in college, I had an incredible, unabashed zeal for the things of the Lord. At other times in my life I have found it laborious even to pray consistently.

Different levels of faith

"Think of yourself with sober judgment, in accordance with the measure of faith God has given you" (Romans 12:3).

"Accept him whose faith is weak" (Romans 14:1).

Though we have all been given a "measure of faith," we all have different portions. I have a friend who will write a check, believing that the money will be in the bank by the time it is cashed. He is a man of great faith. I'll wait till the money's there.

Sin

We are even called upon to "wait for" someone and show patience toward him, even in the area of sin. Consider the patience of God relative to our waywardness: "He [the Lord] is patient with you, not wanting anyone to perish, but everyone to come to repentance (2 Peter 3:9). "Or do you show contempt for the riches of his kindness, tolerance and patience, not realizing that God's kindness leads you toward repentance" (Romans 2:4)?

Two Extremes to Avoid and a Balance to Achieve

There are two extremes to avoid and a balance to achieve when Waiting for One Another.

Two extremes

1. When relating to someone who is slower and who has less capacity, we will be tempted to say, "I want to go faster and do more things—don't hold me back."

2. When relating to someone who is faster and who has more capacity, we will be tempted to say, "Your speed and complexity intimidates and frustrates me—slow down and operate at my speed."

The balance

Wait for One Another is balanced by Honor One Another (Romans 12:10). One way in which we honor someone is to recognize his unique strengths, talents, and gifts and allow him to use them. We should strive to understand the unique contribution that each person can make, acknowledge his or her potential, and then provide the opportunity for that person to function in his or her strength.

For instance, Jesus was not able to do many miracles in his hometown because "Only in his home town and in his own house is a prophet *without honor*" (Matthew 13:57; emphasis added). The people of Nazareth did not recognize Jesus (honor him) for who he was—the Son of God. Therefore he was not able to be who he was and do what he did best among them.

Wait for One Another is balanced by Honor One Another.

So when we're in a relationship in which we are faster and have more capacity, we should be willing to *wait for* the other person:

- *I will gladly wait for you when I need to.*
- *I will not expect you to function at my speed or capacity.*
- *I will not make you feel inferior because we are at different speeds and capacities.*

But when we're in a relationship in which someone is faster and has more capacity, we should be willing to *honor* the other person:

- *I affirm the fact that you can move more quickly and handle more tasks than I can. I want to honor you in your strength.*
- *I don't expect you to always adjust to my speed, but when you do, I feel especially blessed and grateful.*

I once counseled a married couple whose main relational struggle was in this area of waiting and honoring. He was a classic Type-A overachiever; she was not. One particular area of conflict was the fact that she was always running late; she just had a hard time keeping pace. My advice to him was, "Sir, you must wait for your wife. Be patient and gentle. Quit making her feel badly about herself when she's late or when she's slower than you." My advice to her was, "Ma'am, your husband is a very competent person. Honor him. Ask him to help you structure your time and schedule so you can be more punctual and more productive."

The combination of Wait for One Another and Honor One Another transformed their marriage.

List four of your closest relationships. As you consider each one, are you most often called upon to *Wait for* this person or to *Honor* him or her?

Name of person	Wait for or Honor?
_____	_____
_____	_____
_____	_____
_____	_____

Being versus Doing

If we continually struggle with waiting for others, it may be because we're focusing too much on *what people do* rather than concentrating on *who they are*. It's viewing people as *human beings* as opposed to *human doers*.

Here are some principles regarding the balance between the two:

1. Every person has intrinsic value and worth—we are human *beings*.
   - Christ died for everyone (2 Corinthians 5:15).
   - Everyone is created in the image of God (Genesis 1:27).
   - All are crowned in glory and honor (Psalm 8:5).
   - Everyone is unique (Psalm 139:14).
   - We all have great value (Matthew 16:26).

2. Every person should faithfully fulfill what God has called us to do—we are human *doers*.
   - "The Lord has assigned to each his task" (1 Corinthians 3:5).
   - Everyone is responsible for God-given talents and abilities (Matthew 25:1-30).
   - We should all be good workers (Colossians 3:23).
   - We should all live productive lives (Titus 3:14).

3. There should be a proper balance between seeing people as human *beings* and human *doers*.

   If we focus exclusively on what people *do*, their ability to produce, we put them on a performance basis. As long as they produce to our level of expectation, we value them. This is not good.

   If we focus solely on the *being* side of the equation we may encourage apathy, slothfulness and underachievement.

4. In our relationships at home and at church, we should focus mainly on the human *being* side of the equation; at work there can be a legitimate (but balanced) focus on the human *doing* side of the equation.

5. Our lives should be filled with relationships (being) and work (doing).

6. To feel good about ourselves, we need to accept *who we are* (human beings) and then accomplish what God has called us to *do* (our tasks in life).

7. To properly relate to others, we need to concentrate on who they are (human beings) and help them do all that God has called them to do.

8. However, the most important thing is *who we are*, not *what we do*.

Often, when we struggle with Wait for One Another and Bear with One Another, we're probably focusing too much on the doing aspect and need to concentrate instead on the intrinsic value of each human being.

Consider your closest family members. Does your approval of them depend on their performance, or do you concentrate on affirming them simply for who they are?

_____

_____

The Value of Waiting

There is great value in learning to Wait for One Another.

1. Waiting serves as a checks-and-balance system.

I have often prided myself in being able to handle many tasks simultaneously and in completing my work quickly. I also have a corresponding weakness: I'm often impulsive, naive, and quick to start something but slow to finish. Many times in my marriage I have been impatient with Mary because she was unwilling to embrace my spontaneous and multitudinous dreams and visions. I used to think that she was holding me back. In retrospect, 80 percent of those dreams were rash, impulsive decisions that would have fizzled out. I'm glad the Lord has provided Mary as a "governor," a control mechanism in my life. She serves as a checks-and-balances system in my life.

2. Waiting helps us focus on more important issues.

More times than not, when I am impatient (that is, I am being called upon to Wait for One Another but I'm reluctant to do so), it's because I'm focused on a task—a job that needs to get done. I'm seldom tempted with impatience when it comes to people issues. For instance, in my opening illustration regarding the trip to New York—I was more focused on seeing the Empire State Building than on meeting the needs of the older lady in our group.

But when we slow down, we have the time and the inclination to focus on the most important thing—people.

3. Waiting frees people to be comfortable with who they are.

When we are impatient towards people, we are actually being critical of who they are. We make them feel inferior and inadequate. This fosters feelings of condemnation; they begin to feel badly about themselves. But when we wait for people, we affirm who they are and demonstrate acceptance of how they are made.

4. Waiting is a practical way to demonstrate our love to others.

Do you remember the Bible story about the time when God told the Israelites to enter the Promised Land? Prior to leading the nation in, Moses sent twelve men to explore the land. When they returned, ten of the men gave a pessimistic report. Their bottom line was, "We can't do it." Two of the men, Joshua and Caleb, said just the opposite: "God has given us the land, we can do it!" The people chose to listen to the ten pessimists so they wandered in the desert for forty years.

- Why did the ten spies have to wander for forty years? Because of unbelief.
- Why did the entire nation wander for forty years? Because they believed a bad report.
- Why did Joshua and Caleb wander for forty years? Because they wanted to be with the people they loved—they were willing to wait.

Why did Joshua and Caleb wander for forty years?
Because they wanted to be with the people they loved-they were willing to wait.

Another Trip to New York City

It's been said that what goes around, comes around. I began this chapter by relating the story of my trip to New York City and being called upon to "wait for" an older lady in our tour group. Two years after this incident, I was again in New York City, this time with a group of students.

A week before the trip, I was diagnosed with a stress fracture in my left foot. The doctor put a removable cast on my foot that made walking uncomfortable, awkward—and slow.

I remember the moment it occurred to me that now *I* was the slow one, in need of people waiting for me. We were walking down Fifth Avenue and suddenly I was left behind. I felt neglected, inferior, and had I not known the city well, I would have been frightened.

For seven days *I* was the slow one.

Occasionally, a member of the group would make a conscientious effort to break stride with the group, slow down to my pace, and accompany me. During those times, I felt cared for and loved. I remember in particular, an athletic student who "died to self," slowed down, and stayed with me while his friends rushed ahead. He may not have realized that he was obeying 1 Corinthians 11:33 (Wait for One Another) and that in a practical way he was demonstrating love to me, but he was.

This incident reminded me again of the reciprocal aspect of the One Anothers. We need to give them to others, but there will always come a time in our lives when we need to receive them as well.

Final Thoughts

Earlier in this chapter, I referred to the apostle Paul's discussion of ministering to the weaker parts of the body (1 Corinthians 12). Verse 22 says, "those parts of the body that seem to be weaker are indispensable." Notice the word *indispensable*. I always thought that the weaker parts were simply to be tolerated, patronized, and endured. But Paul says that they are essential. I must admit, I don't understand the depth of this truth, but I do accept it. I can't function properly without the weaker parts of the body.

But I also believe that *how I respond to the weaker parts is very important to God* and that *it may be a clear indication as to whether or not the love of God is being poured out through my life*.

The following story illustrates my point:

Chush is a school in Brooklyn, New York, that caters to learning-disabled children. Some children remain in Chush for their entire school career, while others can eventually be mainstreamed into conventional schools.

At a Chush fund-raising dinner, a father told a story about his son, named Shay. It was a story that would never be forgotten by any who attended.

One afternoon, Shay and his father walked past a park where some boys Shay knew were playing baseball. Shay asked, "Do you think they will let me play?" Shay's father knew that his son was not at all athletic and that most boys would not want him on their team. But Shay's father understood that if his son were chosen to play it would give him a comfortable sense of belonging.

Shay's father approached one of the boys in the field and asked if Shay could play. The boy looked around for guidance from his teammates. Getting none, he took matters into his own hands and said, "We're losing by six runs and the game is in the eighth inning. I guess he can be on our team, and we'll try to put him up to bat in the ninth inning."

Shay's father was ecstatic as Shay smiled broadly. Shay was told to put on a glove and go out to play short center field. In the bottom of the eighth inning, Shay's team scored a few runs but was still behind by three. In the bottom of the ninth inning, Shay's team scored again, and now there were two outs, bases loaded, and the potential winning run on base. Shay was scheduled to be up. Would the team actually let Shay bat at this juncture and give away their chance to win the game?

Surprisingly, Shay was given the bat. Everyone knew that it was all but impossible because Shay didn't even know how to hold the bat properly, let alone hit with it. However as Shay stepped up to the plate, the pitcher moved a few steps to lob the ball in softly so Shay should at least be able to make contact. The first pitch came and Shay swung clumsily and missed. One of Shay's teammates came up to Shay and together they held the bat and faced the pitcher waiting for the next pitch. The pitcher again took a few steps forward to toss the ball softly toward Shay. As the pitch came in, Shay and his teammate swung at the ball and together they hit a slow ground ball to the pitcher.

The pitcher picked up the soft grounder and could easily have thrown the ball to the first baseman. Shay would have been out and that would have ended the game. Instead, the pitcher took the ball and threw it on a high arc to right field, far beyond reach of the first baseman. Everyone started yelling, "Shay, run to first. Run to first." Never in his life had Shay run to first. He scampered down the baseline, wide-eyed and startled. By the time he reached first base, the right fielder had the ball. He could have thrown the ball to the second baseman, who would tag out Shay, who was still running. But the right fielder understood what the pitcher's intentions were, so he threw the ball high and far over the third baseman's head. Everyone yelled, "Run to second, run to second." Shay ran toward second base as the runners ahead of him deliriously circled the bases toward home.

As Shay reached second base, the opposing shortstop ran to him, turned him in the direction of third base, and shouted, "Run to third." As Shay rounded third, the boys from both teams ran behind him, screaming, "Shay, run home." Shay ran home, stepped on home plate, and all eighteen boys lifted him on their shoulders and made him the hero, as if he had just hit a "grand slam" and won the game for his team.

"That day," said the father softly with tears now rolling down his face, "those eighteen boys demonstrated to my son, God's perfect love."

God is watching us. How *will* we treat the "weaker members" of his body? God has allowed us to be channels of his love. Perhaps there is no purer demonstration of his love flowing through us than when we wait for and bear with, weaker members of his body.

Every member of the body of Christ is important. Every member must be honored and cared for.

Personal Journal

1. Write about a time in your life when someone waited for you.

   _____

   _____

2. Write about a time when you waited for someone else.

   _____

   _____

3. Write about a time in the past when you should have waited for someone but did not.

   _____

   _____

4. Are you a patient person? How does this relate to your ability to "wait for" and "bear with" others?

   _____

   _____

5. Consider again, how Wait for One Another and Honor One Another can provide balance in a relationship. Which of the two are you called upon to do the most? Or, put another way, which of the two do you struggle with the most?

   _____

6. Write your own definition of Wait for One Another.

   _____

   _____

7. On a scale from 1 to 10 (1 being, "I need to improve" and 10 being, "I do a good job"), how well do you do at waiting for others?

   I rate myself a _____.

Group Time

Each member of the group should give his or her individual response to the first two questions. Allow about two minutes for each person's response. Allow all group members to share answers to question #1 before proceeding to question #2.

1. What was the most interesting concept in this chapter?
2. Share your responses to the first three Personal Journal questions.

As a group, process these discussion questions. The discussion questions have been prioritized. Depending on the time allotted for your group discussion, you may not be able to discuss all the questions.

  a. Read Colossians 3:12 and notice the "clothing" we are to wear. Discuss each garment and how it relates to Wait for One Another.
  b. What are some common excuses for our impatience? Why are none of these excuses valid?
  c. Read 1 Corinthians 12:22. Why are the weaker parts of the body of Christ indispensable?
  d. Read Psalm 41:1-3 and discuss God's reward for those who regard the weak.
  e. Should we be willing to wait for someone who is slothful or lazy?
  f. Read Romans 15:1 and comment on the last phrase.

HONOR ONE ANOTHER

"Honor one another" (Romans 12:10).

We can Honor One Another in various ways.

I respect you.

"Show proper respect to everyone" (1 Peter 2:17).

1. Before I make a decision that will affect your life, I'm going to ask for your opinion and seriously consider your input.

I remember the day I informed my wife that God had called us to another church (which happened to be in another city) so we would be relocating our lives and ministry. Notice the phrase, "I informed my wife." This was wrong and hurtful. Was God, indeed, calling us to a new work? Yes. But I was still wrong. Did God eventually bless the new work? Yes. But I was still wrong.

Why was I wrong? Because, as a matter of respect, before I made a decision that would affect Mary's life I should have asked her opinion and seriously considered her input.

In some instances, we may not always be obligated to *abide* by other people's opinion, but we should always seek it and treat it seriously. In a marriage relationship, take that one step further—we *must* solicit our spouse's opinion and only under extreme circumstances should we continue unless we are in total agreement.

Consider this principle in the context of leadership and decision-making in the local church. How often does a pastor *announce* to the church, a major initiative? If he is making a decision that will affect many lives but neglecting to solicit their input, he is acting disrespectfully.

The more important a decision is, the more necessary it is to get other people's input. For instance, relative to family decisions, the decision to relocate to another city is more important than where the next vacation will be, which is more important than the plans for the weekend, which is more important than which dessert Mom will make for supper. However, respect is always appreciated on any level.

What was the last major decision you made? Did you properly consult everyone who was affected by your decision?

2. *I will respect the things that you feel strongly about.*

I'm not a neat person. I've never understood why one should have to make the bed in the morning—it's going to get messed up again soon, so why bother? To me, there's nothing wrong with taking off your blue jeans and throwing them over a chair—a convenient, accessible location. Coat hangers are a waste of resources. Dirty clothes should just be thrown in the corner of the room.

But I work with a man who considers neatness next to godliness (though he has never been able to provide a substantiating scripture). His office is always neat, his house is immaculate, and his personage well kept. We recently roomed together on a mission trip to NYC. He joined the group three days into the trip.

The day he arrived I surveyed our room - bed unmade, clothes draped over the furniture, dirty clothes piled in the corner. It occurred to me that my messiness would bother my friend, so, out of respect for him I straightened up the room.

3. *I will respect that which belongs to you - your privacy, property, and time.*
- I will knock on your door and ask permission to enter your room.
- I will not intrude on you when you need privacy.
- If I borrow something that belongs to you, I will take care of it, be responsible for it, and return it to you.
- I will respect your time by not being late, realizing that when you have to wait on me, I am robbing you of a precious commodity—time.

I recognize and affirm who you are—your gifts and talents.
"We have different gifts, according to the grace given us" (Romans 12:6).

Strive to understand the unique contribution that each person can make and then acknowledge that potential and help provide the opportunity for each person to function in his or her strength.

Jesus was not able to do many miracles in his hometown because "Only in his home town and in his own house is a prophet *without honor*" (Matthew 13:57; emphasis added). The people of Nazareth did not recognize Jesus (honor him) as who he was—the Son of God. Therefore he was not able to be who he was and do what he did best, among them.

To the contrary, when the apostle Paul was shipwrecked on the island of Malta, he wrote that the islanders "honored us in many ways" (Acts 28:10). Therefore, Paul was able to heal the father of Publius, the chief officer of the island, and many others - "The rest of the sick on the island came and were cured" (v. 9).

I have a friend who is a gifted teacher. But in our church his gift was not being honored; his spiritual gift was neglected and he was frustrated. One might suggest, "If someone is that gifted, he should speak up—exert himself—demand a teaching position." But there is no honor in aggressively *taking* a position of honor. Also, that would violate one of the basic principles of the One Anothers—they are best given and not taken. If we must *take* honor, comfort, or encouragement we will not be satisfied. Rather, we must take the initiative to *give* the One Anothers to others. So it was incumbent upon the leadership of the church to recognize, acknowledge, and affirm my friend's gift and to facilitate him using his gift for his own self-fulfillment and for the glory of God.

Before we can truly honor someone, we must *know him intimately*. How can I acknowledge and affirm a person's gifts if I don't even know what those gifts are? And to know someone intimately I must spend quality time with him with the focused intent of discovering his gifts. It's like going on a treasure hunt and the treasure is hidden inside a human being. How has God uniquely blessed this person? What gifts, talents, and skills are lying dormant, waiting to be activated?

Often, an individual may not know himself what his talents and gifts are. For instance, many Christians don't understand spiritual gifts and have never discovered their own special gift. In this case, part of honoring a person is to help him discover his unique resources.

This is a critical role that all parents should play in the lives of their children—helping each child discover his or her gifts. We almost missed it with my youngest daughter. It wasn't until her junior year in high school that we discovered her remarkable talent in drama. Eighteen months later she was accepted into Juilliard and is now on her way to becoming a professional actress. It frightens me to think - *What if we had never discovered her acting ability?* What a frustrating life she would have lived. My daughter would have been "without honor" even among her family (Matthew 13:57).

> Before we can truly honor someone, we must know him intimately.

Sadly, the people we dishonor and neglect the most are often those who are "among us," "in our home town," "among our relatives," and "in our own house." Just as it was in the ministry of Christ, we are often amazed at the abilities of those closest to us and can't figure out where the abilities came from (Matthew 13:54). So we must recognize, acknowledge, and affirm people's talents, gifts, and skills and help facilitate them using their resources for their own self-fulfillment and for the glory of God. If we don't honor people, their gifts and talents may lay dormant and unused, or, they will simply leave. When Jesus was not honored in Nazareth he "went on his way" (Luke 4:30).

Different Types of Resources

- *Talents*—God-given abilities, given at physical birth: music, athletics, drama, leadership, math, writing.
- *Gifts*—God-given abilities, given at spiritual birth: teaching, exhortation, mercy, serving—see Romans 12:6-8.
- *Skills*—Abilities that we have developed through formal or informal education: web master, electrician, graphic design, music.
- *Strengths*—Character traits that we have developed: punctuality, neatness, loyalty.

After each person's name, list some unique resources he or she has and then record a way in which you could honor that person.

	Name	*Unique resource*	*Your attitude toward these gifts*
Your spouse	_____	_____	_____
Your child	_____	_____	_____
A friend	_____	_____	_____
A co-worker	_____	_____	_____

I submit to your authority.

"Submit yourselves for the Lord's sake to every authority instituted among men" (1 Peter 2:13).

The story is told about a married couple who had attended a seminar taught by one of those male demagogues determined to show that Scripture teaches that the man is IN CHARGE at home. It was the kind of terrible teaching on submission that turns women into lowly doormats. Well, the husband just loved it! He had never heard anything like that in his life, and he drank it all in. His wife, however, sat there fuming as she listened to hour after hour of this stuff.

When they left the meeting that night, the husband felt drunk with fresh power as he climbed into the car. While driving home, he said rather pompously, "Well, what did you think about that?" His wife didn't utter a word, so he continued, "I think it was great!"

When they arrived home, she got out and followed him silently into the house. Once inside, he slammed the door and said, "Wait right there-just stand right there." She stood, tight-lipped, and stared at him. "I've been thinking about what the fellow said tonight, and I want you to know that from now on that's the way it's gonna be around here. You got it? That's the way things are gonna run in this house."

And having said that, he didn't see her for two weeks. After two weeks, he could start to see her just a little bit out of one eye.

The topic of submission has become a hot button in our generation because of two misunderstandings:

- Those *in* authority have misunderstood their role, not realizing that they have been placed in authority in order to *serve* others and that the Bible does command mutual submission, "submit to one another" (Ephesians 5:21). This unfortunate and misdirected mind-set produces overbearing, egotistical, narrow-minded, self-serving, domineering leaders.
- Those *under* authority often don't realize that God has indeed established levels of authority and that he will often work his sovereign will through them. This misunderstanding produces rebellious, insolent, oppositional, reluctant, challenging followers.

Despite the imbalance that often exists, the Bible makes it clear that we are to honor (respect) those who are in authority over us (Romans 13:1-7).

List those who are in authority over you. In your heart, and actions, are you submissive to them?

Authority	*Your attitude toward this authority*
_____	_____
_____	_____
_____	_____

I value and esteem you.

"Because you had become so dear to us" (1 Thessalonians 2:8).

Yes, we are to honor people because they are due respect.
Yes, we are to honor people by acknowledging their unique abilities and gifts.
Yes, we are to honor people by submitting to their authority.
But when we honor someone, we should explore and express another dimension - an emotional one, an issue of the heart.

I can give proper respect, acknowledge abilities, and submit to authority but do so simply out of duty and obligation. I can do it because I know I'm supposed to but, at the same time, resent doing it because I don't want to. I may be like the young boy who was made to sit in the corner as punishment for misbehaving who said, "I may be sitting down on the outside, but I'm standing up on the inside."

Honoring others will take us further. We should honor people because of the great value they have as human beings. This is a recurring theme throughout the entire study of the One Anothers. We love others simply because they are objects of God's love, created in his image.

When honoring someone we should be "smiling on the inside"; we should take pleasure in doing so.

I will give you the advantage.

"Honor one another *above yourselves*" (Romans 12:10, emphasis added).

Honoring others often requires that we give them the advantage, that we intentionally prefer others to ourselves.

In the early days of my ministry, a friend of mine and I attended a professional conference together. We were both at the stage in our careers when we wanted to distinguish ourselves among our colleagues, an attitude that, in retrospect, was quite vain and contrary to proper kingdom attitude. But, there we were amongst fifty of our own, trying to establish our value and worth.

During one particular session, the moderator asked my friend to take the floor and comment on a growing trend in our profession. It was quite an opportunity. I'll never forget what happened next. My friend said, "I would enjoy talking about that, but there's someone here who knows a lot more about the subject that I do. I'd like to defer to Don McMinn and let him lead us in the discussion."

My friend's unselfish gesture made a big impact on my life. He preferred me and honored me—above himself.

Honoring others often requires that we give them the advantage, that we intentionally **prefer others to ourselves.**

I will give you special consideration and proper recognition.

"Give proper recognition to those widows who are really in need" (1 Timothy 5:3).
"The parts that we think are less honorable we treat with special honor"
(1 Corinthians 12:23).

One year, I served a church as interim worship leader. It was a wonderful, loving fellowship. There was a mentally challenged young man who sang in the choir. He could not sing on pitch, didn't know how to read music, and was socially awkward.

But I'll never forget how the other choir members honored him. They treated him like he was their fair-haired child, their pride and joy. They went out of their way to greet him, help him, and make him feel comfortable. Often, when he got excited about the music, he would sing loudly - too loudly (remember, he sang off-pitch), but people would just smile and graciously accept him. They did more than merely tolerate him—they honored him and treated him special. They obeyed 1 Corinthians 12:23.

The verse says that when we recognize someone as a "weaker member" (verse 22) we should not neglect him; instead, we should treat him with *special* honor. Weaker members get more honor than the stronger ones.

The Blessing of Honor One Another

1. Honoring is the key to the body of Christ functioning, as it should.

"The body is a unit, though it is made up of many parts; and though all its parts are many, they form one body. Now you are the body of Christ, and each one of you is a part of it (1 Corinthians 12:12, 27).

Just like our physical bodies work best when all the various parts are functioning properly, the spiritual body of Christ is at its best when each member is doing his or her part. Honor one another is a critical part of making this happen.

2. Honoring is the key to maintaining unity among the body.

"But God has combined the members of the body and has given greater honor to the parts that lacked it, *so that there should be no division in the body*, but that its parts should have equal concern for each other" (1 Corinthians 12:24-25, emphasis added).

For the body of Christ to function properly, there must be unity among its members. Kingdom work can't happen where there's strife and division. Other organizations may be able to function without unity, but not the church.

For instance, a restaurant can continue to function even though there is strife among its employees. The maître d' can be mad at the head-waiter, who is upset at the cook, who can't stand the busboy, but as long as each one does his job, the restaurant can function. Not so the body of Christ.

As a minister at a local church, I must be at peace with my fellow staff members and church members. If the pastor is angry with the worship pastor, who can't stand the youth pastor, who is upset at the children's pastor, the church will not function as it should, regardless of how good everyone tries to act.

Honor One Another (along with other One Anothers) is an important part of maintaining peace and unity among the body.

3. Honoring is the key to assimilation.

Assimilation is a buzzword in the church growth/church health area. Basically, it means that when someone joins a church, two things need to happen in the first four months, or the chances are good that he won't stay: (1.) The new member needs to become relationally connected to at least three or four other people, and (2.) The new member needs to become involved in a ministry in which he can use his unique gifts, talents, and skills.

Honor One Another is a key element in becoming involved in ministry and the other thirty-four One Anothers are key in establishing deep relationships.

Have you been properly assimilated into the life of your church? Are you relationally connected to several people? Are you actively involved in a ministry in which you can use your skills?

4. Honoring is the key to self-actualization.

Years ago, a psychologist named Maslow suggested that a critical part of emotional and psychological health depended upon an individual being self-actualized. Every person must discover what he was created to do, and do it. A teacher must teach, a painter must paint, and an organizer must organize. Although Maslow did not approach his theory from a Christian perspective, it really does reflect the teaching of 1 Corinthians 12. God has indeed created each of us to be unique, and he has a distinctive mission for us to accomplish in life. We will not be fully happy until we discover our destiny and live it.

And that, in large part, is what Honor One Another is all about: helping each other find our niche in life, affirming it, and facilitating its fulfillment.

Every person must discover what he was created to do, **and do it.** A teacher must teach, a painter must paint, and an organizer must organize.

Hindrances to Honoring Others

Romans 12 says to "Honor one another *above yourself*" (emphasis added). Any form of selfishness will short-circuit the grace gift of honoring others.

- Territorialism—*I like my turf and don't want anyone else on it.*
- Having to prove my value and worth—*If I honor you, that may diminish the attention and honor I receive.*
- Preoccupation with self—*I'm so focused on me, I am unable to focus on you.*
- Jealousy—*What if I honor you in an area in which we are both involved in and it turns out that you are better at it than I am?*
- Insecurity—*If I honor the strengths of other people, I might expose my own inadequacies.*
- Fear of unmet needs—*If I honor other people, who will honor me?*

Personal Journal

1. Has anyone ever helped you discover and cultivate your gifts and talents? Write about your experience.

   _____

   _____

2. Think about your colleagues at work. Are you willing to honor them above yourself? What would be a practical way of doing that?

   _____

   _____

3. Referring to the list of "hindrances to honoring others," which of these do you struggle with the most?

   _____

4. Do you feel self-actualized? Explain.

   _____

   _____

5. Write your own definition of Honor One Another.

   _____

   _____

6. On a scale from 1 to 10 (1 being, "I need to improve" and 10 being, "I do a good job"), how well do you do at honoring others?

   I rate myself a _____.

Group Time

Each member of the group should give his or her individual response to the first two questions. Allow about two minutes for each person's response. Allow all group members to share answers to question #1 before proceeding to question #2.

1. What was the most interesting concept in this chapter?
2. Share your responses to the first three Personal Journal questions.

As a group, process these discussion questions. The discussion questions have been prioritized. Depending on the time allotted for your group discussion, you may not be able to discuss all the questions.

a. Read Romans 13:7 and discuss the fact that we "owe" people honor.
b. Read 1 Peter 2:17 and discuss the fact that we are to respect *everyone*.
c. Is there ever a case in which someone is dishonorable and therefore not worthy of being honored?

Chapter

4

OFFER HOSPITALITY TO ONE ANOTHER

"Offer hospitality to one another" (1 Peter 4:9).

Alice James, wife of William James, says that often during evenings her husband would exclaim, "Are we never to have an evening alone? Must we always talk to people every night?" And she would answer, "I will see that whoever calls tonight is told that you are busy." So they would settle down to their quiet evening. Soon the doorbell would ring and Alice would go to the entry, making sure that her instructions were carried out. Close behind her would be William, exclaiming, "Come in! Come right in!"

God's people should be hospitable. We should be gracious hosts. We should be generous and cordial to guests and offer a pleasant environment for them.

There's nothing mysterious about this One Another; it is entirely practical. It simply means: Care for people by offering them fellowship and a meal. Be gracious and kind when meeting new people. Fellowship often around drink and a meal.

At one church I served, we developed a simple but effective strategy for the members of a large Bible study class to get to know one another on a deeper level. Since there were one hundred or more members in the class, we asked eleven couples to host a covered-dish dinner in their homes. Then we randomly assigned everyone in the class to a host home. The evening's agenda: Share a meal together, become better acquainted, and then pray for each other. This simple exercise yielded tremendous results: oneness and care for one another increased. We made it a biannual event.

Planned events are good, but our *spirit* of hospitality should be spontaneous and eager. Initially we may need some prodding, but eventually our desire to be hospitable should be natural and unstructured. Our homes should be frequented by friends and strangers (Hebrews 13:2).

In the first twenty years of our marriage, Mary and I seldom had people over to our house. Our guest book had cobwebs on it. It was our loss.

Why did we neglect this blessed ministry? Neither of our parents modeled it for us when we were growing up, no one ever taught us or encouraged us to do it, we were probably too self-oriented to want to be other-people-oriented, and, we just didn't realize what a wonderful ministry it is to offer hospitality to others.

But in the past several years, hardly a month goes by that we don't have at least one, usually two, dinners in our home. Each year we'll have between eighty and one hundred individuals in our home for a time of relaxed but meaningful ministry.

When was the last time you had people in your house for a meal?

_____

There are many ways to show hospitality to others:
- Take people out to eat at a restaurant.
- Provide housing at a local hotel for out-of-town guests.
- Plan a party or reception to honor an individual, couple, or group (birthday, anniversary, graduation).
- Have people in your home for a meal.
- Provide lodging in your home for guests.

Offering hospitality has two main objectives:

1. Graciously providing for the physical needs of others, specifically—food and lodging.
2. Providing an environment in which relationships can be nurtured and developed.

> In the first twenty years of our marriage, Mary and I seldom had people over to our house. Our guest book had cobwebs on it. It was our loss.

In this chapter, we'll focus on one particular expression of sharing hospitality—having people in your home for a meal. I'll concentrate on this aspect for two reasons: nearly everyone can offer this type of hospitality (whereas everyone may not be able to offer housing), and, in the past several years, Mary and I have been particularly blessed by both the giving and receiving of this type of hospitality.

Practical Suggestions

1. Don't worry about the size and condition of your house.

Some people are reluctant to offer hospitality because they live in a modest house or their furniture is sparse or worn. But the benefit of hospitality has nothing to do with the size or quality of your house. The fact that you have invited people into your world is significant. The most important thing is what happens in the hearts of your guests.

However, it _is_ important that your house be clean and that you are prepared for your guests.

What other issues (hindrances, objections, excuses) do we often have to resolve before we will be willing to have people in our home?

_____

_____

2. Plan ahead and give people clear instructions and directions.
- Plan your dinner several weeks in advance.
- Let guests know who else is invited.
- Give people written directions to your house.
- Give specific instructions regarding the time dinner begins, when it will end, whether or not they are expected to bring anything, appropriate dress, your telephone number, and a general agenda for the evening.
- Be clear about whether or not children are invited.

3. Consider carefully the size of your group.
The ministry aspect of offering hospitality *increases* as the number of invited guests *decreases*. Compare the emotional/spiritual difference between inviting one couple to your home to having thirty people in your home. They both qualify as hospitality and both will be appreciated but being one of thirty is entirely different than being one of two.

The ministry aspect of showing hospitality *increases* as the number of invited guests *decreases*.

4. Keep the meal simple.
Remember, the meal that is served is a means to an end, not an end in itself. Physical nourishment is secondary to emotional and spiritual nourishment.

If the meal is complex (multiple courses, elaborate presentation, gourmet menu, etc.), it puts the host under a lot of unnecessary pressure and may make the guests feel uneasy—people will be overly concerned about maintaining proper etiquette, paying proper compliments, etc. The focus should not be on the meal.

When Mary and I have people over for dinner, we usually serve a simple meal consisting of a casserole, salad, bread, and dessert.

5. Make the evening a joint effort among family members.
It's unfair for the burden of cleaning the house before the dinner, preparing and serving the meal, and post-meal cleanup to rest on one person. Married couples should share the task. If your children are old enough to help, involve them in greeting guests and serving the meal. Often, your guests will be blessed to observe multiple people involved in showing hospitality.

A servant's heart can be expressed through simple acts such as refilling people's drinks during the meal.

6. Greet people when they arrive.
Make an effort to greet everyone when they first arrive. If possible, even anticipate their arrival and open the door before they ring the doorbell. Physically greet them with a handshake or hug and say something like, "I'm so glad you are here; please come in and make yourself comfortable."

After taking their purse and coats, introduce your guests to other guests and then offer them a drink. Nametags are often helpful. When everyone is gathered, announce where the bathrooms are located, offer free use of the telephone, and give a brief overview of the evening.

7. During dinner, direct the topics of conversation.

Without some direction, dinner conversation can drift to trivial, meaningless, and even questionable topics. While eating dinner with a group of people one time, we spent twenty minutes talking about an insignificant bit of local news. It really was ridiculous. The purpose of the dinner is for people to become better acquainted and to minister to each other's needs. So, the conversation needs to be directed or else it will drift to who knows where.

If the group is small and sitting at one table, the host can steer and control the conversation by initiating certain topics: "Let's go around the table and have everyone share a little about yourself and your family." or, "Everyone share how you became involved in our church."

Do not ask questions that may be uncomfortable for some guests. For instance, I wouldn't suggest, "Everyone share how you came to know Christ" unless I was sure that everyone was a Christian and everyone was comfortable sharing their faith. Likewise, I wouldn't suggest, "Everyone share where you're going on vacation this year" if I knew that someone in the group is unemployed and probably can't afford a vacation.

Usually, general topics are safe because people can choose what and how much they what to share. Topics like, "Where's home for you?" or, "Tell us about your family." are usually safe.

If you're hosting a large group, pre-select table hosts who are prepared with specific instructions, or, simply write the topics on a sheet of paper and give a copy to each group. Before introducing specific topics, allow five to ten minutes for people to settle in and establish contact with those sitting next to them.

8. Control most of the conversation.

As the host, you may need to facilitate a good balance in two areas:

Don't let anyone dominate the dinner conversation. Generally speaking, the conversation should be equally divided among the guests. This is another reason it's a good idea to have pre-selected topics which everyone is asked to respond to. If you say, "Let's go around the table and everyone share where you were born." it will be hard for one person to dominate the conversation.

If someone is talking too much, some subtle phrases can help steer the conversation:

- *John, that's very interesting; let's hear Susan's thoughts.*
- *John, hold that thought. Susan, what is your answer to this question?*
- *John, let's go on around the circle and get everyone's thoughts.*
- *We're about to run out of time on this issue, but we want to hear from everyone. Susan, what do you think?*

If someone is not participating much she could be encouraged to talk by saying:

- *Jill, what would be your response to this issue?*
- *Jill, what do you think about what Susan said?*

Try not to spend the entire conversation talking about only one or two topics. First, you run the risk of over-discussing a topic, and, there may be members of the group who do not enjoy a particular topic or feel that they cannot contribute intelligently to the conversation. (For instance, imagine how out-of-place a non-musician would feel if you spent the entire evening talking about classical music.)

9. After dinner, engage in additional One Anothers.

      Mary and I often combine Offer Hospitality to One Another with Pray for One Another. After dinner, we move to the den, where I share a short devotional on what it means to Pray for One Another. Then I ask each guest (or couple), "How can we pray for you?" and we pray for that individual or couple. I'm careful not to ask anyone to pray aloud unless I know for sure that he is comfortable doing so. It's often good to mention at the beginning that no one will be asked to pray aloud—just to relieve any stress and anxiety.

      Other One Anothers can also be engaged in:

- *Comfort One Another*—Perhaps someone in the group is hurting.
- *Encourage One Another*—Perhaps someone is unemployed and needs encouragement.
- *Teach One Another*—Dinner might be followed by a teaching session.
- *Confess Your Faults to One Another and Forgive One Another*—A group of married couples could be encouraged to spend time making sure that their relationship is "up-to-date" and not hampered by un-confessed sin and unresolved anger.

10. Bring the evening to a proper ending.

      Let people know when it's okay to leave so they can leave without fear of disrupting the evening's agenda by leaving too early. I usually say something like, "Mary and I are so glad that you could come over tonight. Thank you for being here. You can stay longer and fellowship if you wish, or, if you need to slip out now, please do so."

It is around the dinner table that *friends best experience* the **joys of friendship**.

11. As people leave, say a personal good-bye.

Personally affirm each person as he or she leaves. A physical affirmation is appropriate (hug, handshake) as is a verbal one, "I'm so glad you were able to come tonight. Please come again. You are always welcome in our house."

Optional suggestions:

    1. Give each guest a gift.

      A nice touch is to give each guest a small gift. Christian bookstores often have devotional books or gifts on sale for a small price. Other, simple gifts might include: a rose from your garden, the recipe of the meal you served, or a list of the names and address of everyone who attended.

    2. Take pictures.

      Take pictures during the evening (being careful to get at least one picture of each guest) and send individual pictures to each guest along with a personal note.

    3. Encourage others to Offer Hospitality.

      Once you have modeled for people how to Offer Hospitality and they have been blessed by participating, encourage them to give to others by hosting a dinner in their own home.

How to Respond to Someone Who Offers You Hospitality.

1. Graciously receive the invitation and quickly respond with an answer.

2. Offer to bring part of the meal.
3. Be on time.
4. Consider where to park; don't block the driveway or the neighbor's driveway.
5. If appropriate, bring a simple gift and subtly give it to your host.
6. Respect the rules of the house. (Ex. No food in the den. Don't rough-house with the dog.)
7. Respect your host's leadership. For instance, don't hijack the topic of conversation, don't turn on the TV, and, inform your host ahead of time if you must leave early.
8. Don't dominate your host's time.
9. Leave at a decent time.
10. Express gratitude verbally and follow-up with a written note.

Showing hospitality also involves offering your home as a place for people to spend the night, whether for a day or two or an extended time. Here are some suggestions:

1. Married couples should be unified in their offer of hospitality. A guest can usually discern when he or she is welcomed by one spouse but not by the other.
2. Inform everyone in the house about who's coming and how long they will stay.
3. Clearly define how long the houseguest will stay. It's not fair to you or your guests to be unclear in this area.
4. Be clear about your expectations. Will you provide all meals for your guests? Are you expected to entertain them at all times? Will they need transportation?
5. Clearly communicate the house rules. For example: No food in the den; no noise after eleven o'clock at night; don't let the cat outside; let the answering machine pick up all calls; breakfast on your own. Clarify the house rules so your guests will feel comfortable.

Daniel Webster was once bested by one of the farmers of his native state. He had been hunting at some distance from his Inn, and rather than make the long trip back, he approached a farmhouse some considerable time after dark and pounded on the door. An upstairs window was raised and the farmer, with head thrust out, called, "What do you want?"

"I want to spend the night here," said Webster. "All right. Stay there," said the farmer. Down went the window.

Hopefully, our spirit of hospitality will be better.

Personal Journal

1. In recent years, who has offered hospitality to you? _____

2. Among your friends and acquaintances, who do you know who is good at offering hospitality to others? _____

3. In your family of origin, did your parents show hospitality to others? How has this affected your perspective on this ministry?

   _____

   _____

4. Do you frequently offer hospitality to others? If not, why not?

   _____

   _____

5. Write your own definition of Offer Hospitality to One Another.

   _____

   _____

6. On a scale from 1 to 10 (1 being, "I need to greatly improve" and 10 being, "I do a good job"), how well do you offer hospitality to others?

   I rated myself a _____

6. Schedule a time in the near future when you can offer hospitality to others.
   Date _____

   Place _____

   Invitation list _____

Group Time

Each member of the group should give his or her individual response to the first two questions. Allow about two minutes for each person's response. Allow all group members to share their answer to question #1 before proceeding to question #2.

1. What was the most interesting concept in this chapter?
2. Share your responses to the first three Personal Journal entries.

As a group, process these discussion questions: These questions have been prioritized. Depending on the time allotted for your group discussion, you may not be able to process all the questions.

  a. Read and discuss Hebrews 13:2: "Do not forget to entertain strangers, for by so doing some people have entertained angels with knowing it."
  b. Read 1 Peter 4:9 and discuss the last two words, "Offer hospitality to one another *without grumbling.*"
  c. When describing the characteristics of a church leader, the apostle Paul says that an overseer "must be hospitable" (1 Timothy 3:2). Why is this an important part of being a church leader?
  d. Discuss this statement: "It is around the dinner table that friends best experience the joys of friendship."

LIVE IN PEACE WITH ONE ANOTHER

"Live in peace with each other" (1 Thessalonians 5:13).

Related Scriptures:
> "Live in harmony with one another" (1 Peter 3:8).
> "Make every effort to live in peace with all men" (Hebrews 12:14).
> "God has called us to live in peace" (1 Corinthians 7:15).
> "If it is possible, as far as it depends on you, live at peace with everyone" (Romans 12:18).
> "Let us therefore make every effort to do what leads to peace and to mutual edification" (Romans 14:19).

The week I began working on this chapter, I asked the Lord to help me experience this particular One Another so I could learn "how to put it into practice." On Monday morning, three opportunities challenged me:

- A church member was upset because he was not chosen to be on a particular committee.
- Several church members were upset over a song a youth sang in the worship service.
- When listing the members of a mission trip in the church's bulletin, I inadvertently left off someone's name.

At first, I was impatient at having to deal with these issues. I thought:
- *I don't have the time today to resolve these issues.*
- *If these people are upset, let them come to me.*
- *These people just need to grow up.*
- *There are more important things to do in God's kingdom than to put out emotional brush fires.*

But then I was reminded that Scripture tells us to Live in Peace with One Another and that I was to "Make every effort to live in peace with all men" (Hebrews 12:14). The Lord told me:
- that I should do whatever I could do to bring peace in these situations.
- that I should take the initiative to settle these disputes.
- that the time and effort it took to settle these issues was time and effort well spent.
- that dealing with these issues was, indeed, kingdom business.

So I spent about two hours during the first part of the week making calls, setting up meetings, and sending e-mails. By Wednesday, all the fences had been mended, and I had obeyed 1 Thessalonians 5:13.

Before talking about *how to* Live in Peace with One Another, let's lay down some foundational principles.

1. Hurts, offenses and misunderstandings are inevitable.

We are imperfect people living in an imperfect world. Therefore, regardless of how careful we are to avoid hurts and misunderstandings, problems will happen. We should not be shocked or surprised to hear that, "John is upset." We just need to be conscientious enough to pursue resolving the issue.

2. The probability of hurts, offenses, and misunderstandings occurring increases with an increase in activities and the number of people involved.

Proverbs 14:4 says, "Where there are no oxen, the manger is empty, but from the strength of an ox comes an abundant harvest." The "McMinn paraphrase" of this proverb would read: "Where there are no oxen, the manger is clean, but where there are oxen there's going to be some poop that needs to be cleaned up."

Simply stated, whenever you have a group of people (oxen) engaged in numerous activities, there's going to be some relational mishaps. Besides the fact that we're all sinners (which means we're going to inevitably sin against each other), just logistically speaking, whenever a lot of people are involved in numerous tasks, things are going to be overlooked, communication will break down—things are going to mess up. And when that happens, we need to restore the peace.

> Harmony in relationships should take precedence over religious/spiritual activities.

In my church, Sundays and Wednesdays are the busiest days with the most activities involving the most people. So on Monday and Thursday mornings one of the first tasks on my to-do-list is—get out the pooper-scooper and clean up.

Hurts and misunderstandings are just a part of life so we must anticipate the need to make peace and then do it.

What are the busiest, most involved times of your life? (Consider both weekly and annual events.) _____

Do relational challenges usually escalate during these times? _____

3. We should take the initiative to restore the peace.

Jesus said, "Therefore, if you are offering your gift at the altar and there remember that your brother has something against you, leave your gift there in front of the altar. First go and be reconciled to your brother; then come and offer your gift" (Matthew 5:23).

Notice several things about this scripture:
1. Harmony in relationships should take precedence over religious/spiritual activities.
2. If we know that a relationship has been harmed, we should take the initiative to reconcile.
3. We should take the initiative even if it is another person who is upset at us, not just when we are upset.

Many times, knowing that a relationship has been breached, I have thought to myself, *"If he's upset at me, he should call me; he knows my telephone number."* But we are told to be proactive.

When was the last time you took the initiative to resolve a challenging issue that someone else had against you?

_____

_____

4. We should "settle matters quickly" (Matthew 5:25).

Whenever there is a misunderstanding, the matter usually gets worse the longer it is left unresolved. Controversies and misunderstandings seldom evaporate - they usually just go deep into the heart, lie dormant, fester, and begin to poison the soul.

Issues need to be dealt with - and the quicker the better.

Of course, we must be sensitive to the appropriate time and place to have "restoration meetings." For instance, if you're upset at your pastor, don't approach him ten minutes before the worship service.

5. Distinguish between issues that you just need to "drop" and issues that should be addressed.

If taken to an extreme, Live in Peace with One Another can actually have an unsettling effect. If I feel compelled to comment on every minor irritation that comes my way, I'll spend half of my life stirring up the relational waters. Some issues just need to be forgiven, forgotten, and dropped.

For instance, one day I had plans to go to lunch with two colleagues. They usually call me when its time to go eat, and 80 percent of the time we go to the local cafeteria for lunch. On this particular day, they went on down to the cafeteria without calling me. About ten minutes later, I realized that they had left, drove down to the café and, indeed, they were halfway though the line.

Technically, they should have called. I was slightly bothered. But, I realized that these two men love me; they are cordial and considerate men, and no offense was intended. I just needed to drop it. It would have been unnecessary and trite to have made an issue of it.

But note - this word of advice (some issues need to be dropped) applies only to our *personal* issues. If someone else is upset, we can't dismiss the issue as unimportant or too small. We should never dismiss as trivial another person's feelings: "Yeah, I know Bob's upset about being surprised at the meeting, but that's not a big deal, he just needs to drop it."

Do you have difficulty in dropping issues? Give a recent example of having done so.

_____

_____

6. It is our responsibility to "make every effort" to live at peace with people (Romans 14:19), but sometimes our effort will not bring about the desired result.

One day, at church, I offended someone by inadvertently leaving his name off the church bulletin (he was part of an ensemble that sang in the service). If that had happened to me, I wouldn't have been offended, but it really bothered him. I approached him after the service and sincerely apologized, but I could tell my apology didn't bring peace. I called the next morning, reached his voice mail, and again apologized and asked his forgiveness. But he was still upset. At that point, I had done everything I could do; I had "made every effort." Of course, I'll continue to pray for him and the situation, I'll go out of my way to show kindness and care for him, and I'll be more careful in the future to make sure it doesn't happen again...but for the moment, I've made every effort. Emotionally, I should feel free to go on.

7. At times, we may be called upon to help arbitrate other people's quarrels and misunderstandings.

"I plead with Euodia and I plead with Syntyche to agree with each other in the Lord. Yes, and I ask you, loyal yokefellow, help these women who have contended at my side in the cause of the gospel" (Philippians 4:2-3).

[Consider also, that the entire book of Philemon was Paul's attempt to mediate a dispute between Philemon and Onesimus.]

The admonition to Live in Peace with One Another certainly applies to us whenever we have a dispute with someone or when someone has an issue with us, but in certain cases we also have an obligation to intervene in situations in which we are not personally involved.

Initially, this might involve encouraging someone to take action – "John, I really think that you and Bob need to get together and talk out your differences." At times, we may need to get directly involved – "John, let me set up a meeting with you, Bob, and me so that this issue can be settled."

Helping others Live in Peace is certainly the responsibility of those in authority:

- Parents should take the initiative to help their children correctly handle conflict in their relationships.
- Church leaders should protect the unity of the body by encouraging and/or initiating conflict resolution among church members.
- Employers have the right to get involved in relational conflicts that affect their business environment.

8. Peace and harmony among the body of Christ are very important to God.

Live in Peace with One Another is a big deal with God. [See 1 Corinthians 7:15, Colossians 3:15, and Ephesians 4:3] Perhaps the climatic statement of Jesus' high priestly prayer was the phrase, "that they may be one as we are one" (John 17:22). Christ wants his body to be united, to live in harmony, to be at peace, and not to be torn by strife and division. That's why we must continually work at keeping the peace with others.

Ephesians 4:15—A Key Concept in Making Peace with Others

"Speak the truth in love" (Ephesians 4:15). These five words provide a practical strategy for maintaining healthy relationships.

There are three keys to obeying this verse.

Speak.

When there is misunderstanding or strife in a relationship, it needs to be discussed. Both parties need to talk. Regardless of the emotion (anger, disappointment, frustration, confusion), both parties need to verbalize their feelings and thoughts. We may think that the spiritually mature thing to do is to be quiet, to swallow hard and just "take it." But the apostle Paul says to *speak*.

In every relationship, there should be the freedom to speak. Every marriage, friendship, family relationship, and work relationship should have that freedom. In any relationship, if one person feels intimidated about speaking out, the relationship is unhealthy.

Here are two suggestions on how to make this work in every relationship.

1. Be approachable.

To keep relationships healthy, we need to be approachable. Let others know that they are welcome to approach you when needed. Give them permission to share the truth in love with you by saying something like this: "When I do something that hurts you, or if you misunderstand something I do or say, please come to me and tell me what you're thinking. I promise to receive you and listen to what you have to say."

To be approachable doesn't mean you must change your mind or position to agree with whomever is approaching you. Even after they speak the truth in love you may feel compelled to maintain your conviction or even defend yourself. But being approachable means that people know that they can communicate with you.

Becoming approachable has nothing to do with lines of authority. We should never convey the message, "I'm the father, and you're the child. Don't ever confront me with an issue," or, "I'm the boss, you're my employee. You don't have the right to approach me, even if I'm wrong."

In an effort to become more approachable, visit with your family members, close friends and co-workers and give them permission to speak to you when you hurt them or when there is a misunderstanding.

2. Be a good listener.

The admonition to speak also implies that the person who is being spoken to should *listen*. Someone has defined listening as, "the time I waste hearing you while I plan my next response." For many people that's all it is. Perhaps that's why Luke 8:18 says, "Therefore consider carefully how you listen."

Patricia Golaman, the vice chairman of the National Transportation Safety Board, tells a story about a stewardess who, frustrated by passenger inattentiveness during her what-to-do-in-an-emergency talk at the beginning of each flight, changed the wording and said, "When the mask drops down in front of you, place it over your navel and continue to breathe normally." Not a single passenger noticed.

Do you ever feel like no one's listening to you? On the flip side, are you a good listener?

In every relationship, there should be the freedom to speak. Every marriage, friendship, parent/child relationship and work relationship should **have that freedom.**

Here are some biblical perspectives on how to be a good listener.

Listen More. *"Everyone should be quick to listen, slow to speak"* (James 1:19).

It's been said that a picture is worth a thousand words, but some people still prefer the thousand words – they talk too much. When someone is "speaking the truth in love" to you, close your mouth and *listen*.

Listen Carefully. *"You will be ever hearing but never understanding"* (Matthew 13:14).

Have you ever been talking to someone, really sharing your heart, but you can tell that he's not really focused on what you're saying? During your conversation he looks around at other people, reads the paper, or fiddles with a pen. Or maybe he looks at you with a far-away look in his eyes. Frustrating, isn't it?

To be a good listener, listen carefully; focus on the person who is sharing and concentrate on what he is saying. Give people your undivided attention even when you're listening to them on the phone.

Listen to what the person is saying from her heart, not just from her mouth. *"Out of the overflow of the heart the mouth speaks"* (Matthew 12:34).

Sometimes people don't mean what they say, but sometimes people mean more than what they say. Learn to listen intently, not only to people's words, but also to their heart. According to Matthew 12:34, when we talk we're exposing our heart. If a person says, "I can't do anything right," his heart may be saying, "I need you to encourage me. I'm feeling insecure." If your friend says, "I need some time off," he may be going through a difficult time; he may be facing more difficulties than he's willing to talk about. When a teenager says, "I just want to go to my room," that may mean that something hurtful happened at school. Listening is the quickest way to see inside the soul of another human and to discern his needs.

Listen and Remember. *"Not forgetting what he has heard"* (James 1:25).

We may do a decent job of listening, but when we leave the conversation we forget what was said. We fall prey to the "out-of-sight, out-of-mind" syndrome. If your spouse or other significant person shares with you his or her fears about a particular issue, what will be your long-term response to this shared information? To listen with remembrance means that the information shared will remain important to you and that you'll be particularly sensitive to your friend in that area. In other words, what you heard will eventually affect your behavior. What you heard may need to be added to your prayer list and prayed for regularly.

Do you ever feel like no one's listening to you? On the flip-side, *are you a good listener?*

Speak the *truth*.

When we speak, we must be careful to speak only the truth. While most of us wouldn't tell a bold-faced lie, we may be tempted to *distort* the facts, *exaggerate* the facts, make *assumptions* (it's been said that assumption is the lowest form of knowledge), or only speak *part of the truth* (naturally, that part which substantiates our position). Instead, share *only* the truth and *all* of the truth. At times, this may require *pursuing* the truth—investigating the details of a situation to make sure all your information is correct.

Proverbs 18:17 says, "The first to present his case seems right, till another comes forward and questions him." Which simply means, there's usually two sides to every story. So it is always wise to get all the facts involving a particular incident. Sometimes we may be upset over something because we're misinformed. Often, just talking out a situation -getting the facts - will resolve the issue.

Speak the truth *in love*.

Some people think that, "armed with the truth," they have a "007 license to kill." They think they can express themselves any way they want, even if it hurts another person. But we can't do that; we must share the truth *in love*.

Do you remember at the first of this chapter I shared about the incident when the teenager sang a song in church and the song was somewhat questionable? On Monday I received two e-mails. They demonstrate the difference between sharing the truth in love and sharing in a blunt, coarse manner:

Email #1 - Awful!! Not worshipful. Not vocally correct in any way. Ruined the service for me. Wondering if you ever preview solos before the rest of us are subjected to them? Please reply.

Email #2—I have always considered myself reasonably tolerant of the worship music that is presented in church. I greatly appreciate some of the modern music that is being sung. However…I'm sorry to tell you that I was very disappointed with the closing music in yesterday's service. We love you.

Here are some suggestions as to what sharing the truth *in love* may involve.

1. *Love must be the motivation behind our sharing.*
   Are we sharing in order to get even, to vent our anger, to humiliate or dispense shame, to be vindictive or hurtful—or is our motivation purely that of love? Do we want to edify the listener or tear him down? Do we want to bring peace to the body of Christ or discord?

2. *Consider what "in love" means for each significant person in your life* so when you *share the truth* with him, you'll know the proper time, place, and approach. In other words, everyone has his own personal criteria as to what "in love" means. Here are some options:
   I want you to speak the truth in love to me, but…
   - *not as soon as I get home from work.*
   - *not in front of the kids.*
   - *not before intimate/sexual encounters.*
   - *not by raising your voice at me.*
   - *not in front of other people.*
   - *not by condemning me; don't attack who I am.*
   - *allow me to share my side of the story.*
   - *not when I'm tired.*
   - *not on Sundays, particularly not before worship services.*
   - *try to understand what I'm saying, even if it doesn't come out in a logical way.*

How would you define what "speaking the truth in love" means to you?

_____

_____

Consider a close family member or friend. How might this person define "speaking the truth in love" for himself or herself?

_____

_____

Other Suggestions

When speaking the truth in love, follow these suggestions:

- Get to the point quickly; don't draw out the conversation or build it up to be larger than life.
- Stick to the issue at hand; don't introduce unrelated issues.
- Speak only to those who are directly involved in the situation. For example, if someone has offended you, to share your thoughts with someone other than your offender would be wrong, even though you may be "speaking the truth in love."
- After speaking the truth, give the person you're talking to an opportunity to respond. Ephesians 4:15 does not give you permission to verbally dump on someone and then leave. Rather, it should be the beginning of a *dialogue* between both parties.
- Be sensitive about *when* you share. Ephesians 4:29 defines unwholesome words as words spoken in an untimely manner.
- Be sensitive about *how* you share. Use a gentle tone of voice; even your body language should be calm and non-intimidating.

Which of the three key elements of Ephesians 4:29 (*speak*, speak *truth*, speak the truth *in love*) are you most often tempted to violate?

_____

Why? _____

The periodical, Christian Victory, recorded that only eight percent of the time since the beginning of recorded history has the world been at peace. In over 3,100 years, only 286 have been warless and during that time 8,000 treaties have been broken. World peace is a myth. That doesn't mean we shouldn't hope for it and make an effort to achieve it, but in reality it's not going to happen.

But we can legitimately anticipate and enjoy relational, interpersonal peace. Yes, it will take constant effort to maintain peace in relationships but it's worth the effort.

Personal Journal

1. When was the last time you made an "effort to be at peace with all men"?

_____

_____

2. When was the last time you should have made the effort but did not?

_____

3. When was the last time someone else initiated this effort toward you?

_____

4. Personality wise, are you reticent to be confrontational, to engage in a controversial issue? Why is it often necessary to play this role?

_____

5. Write your own definition of Live in Peace with One Another.

_____

_____

6. On a scale from 1 to 10 (1 being, "I need to improve" and 10 being, "I do a good job"), how well do you do at Living in Peace with One Another?

I rated myself a _____ .

Group Time

Each member of the group should give his or her individual response to the first two questions. Allow about two minutes for each person's response. Allow all group members to share answers to question #1 before proceeding to question #2.

1. What was the most interesting concept in this chapter?
2. Share your responses to the first three Personal Journal questions.

As a group, process these discussion questions. The discussion questions have been prioritized. Depending on the time allotted for your group discussion, you may not be able to discuss all the questions.

a. When considering how to Live in Peace with One Another, is it ever advisable to act as a third party to two parties who are at odds with each other? Should we ever take the initiative to help bring peace into a situation in which we are not personally involved?

b. One of the foundational principles of the One Anothers is that Christ has first given each one to us so that we can, in turn, give them to others. Discuss the fact that Christ took the initiative to make peace with us (the human race). [See Ephesians 2:12-14.]

c. In this chapter we mentioned the fact that unity among the body of Christ is very important to God. Why is this true?

CARE FOR ONE ANOTHER
"Have the same care one for another" (1 Corinthians 12:25 KJV).

Mamie made frequent trips to the branch post office. One day she encountered a long line of people who were waiting for service. Since Mamie only needed stamps, a helpful observer suggested, "Why don't you use the stamp machine? You can get all the stamps you need, and you won't have to stand in line." Mamie replied, "I know, but the machine can't ask me about my arthritis."

People want to be cared for.

Care for One Another—The First Step in Building Healthy Relationships
In many ways, caring for one another is the foundational building block of all relationships. The old adage, "I don't care how much you know until I know how much you care" is true. To this one old adage, we could add others:
- "I'm not going to be vulnerable with you unless I know you care for me."
- "I'm not going to trust you unless I'm sure you care for me."
- "You may be very competent, knowledgeable, and experienced, but how are you going to treat me?"
- "If you're trying to lead me, I'm not sure I will be willing to follow unless you first convince me that you care for me."

When I am beginning a new friendship, I attempt to discover ways in which I can show my new friend that I care for him or her. It may take up to nine months to establish this dimension of the relationship. Often, a series of simple actions can help establish a progressive growth in this area. For instance, take your new friend to lunch, visit him in his home, invite him to your house, send him a birthday card, call him to see how his week is going, be available to help him in practical ways, be kind to his wife and children, send him a postcard when you go on vacation, send him a newspaper article that he would enjoy reading, or buy him a book about one of his hobbies.

The Apostle Paul's Analogy—The Body of Christ/Our Physical Body
In his writings to the churches at Rome, Corinth, and Ephesus, Paul creates an analogy between the physical human body and the spiritual body of Christ.

In 1 Corinthians 12, Paul uses this analogy extensively. The three verses from which we get the admonition to Care for One Another read, "But God has combined the members the body and has given greater honor to the parts that lacked it, so that there should be no division in the body, but that its parts should have equal concern for each other. If one part suffers, every part suffers with it; if one part is honored, every part rejoices with it" (1 Corinthians 12:24–26).

From these verses, we can learn the following truths about how the body of Christ, the church, functions and demonstrates care to its members:

1. When one part of my body is in pain, it affects the other parts.

Physical body—About once a year, my back is strained. There seems to be no reason for it. Last year I simply picked up a rake in the back yard, and—*snap*—my back gave out. With much discomfort, I made it up the stairs, fell in bed, and convalesced for several days. Although only one part of my body ached, the pain affected every part. My feet couldn't function properly because of my back pain, my hands were inhibited from normal tasks, and my entire body was incapacitated.

Body of Christ—I just received an e-mail from a lifelong friend whose wife has been diagnosed with terminal melanoma. The doctors have given her six months to live. I am saddened by the news. I hurt for my friend. His pain is my pain.

2. When one part of the body is cared for, all parts are affected.

Physical body—Years ago I took one of my daughters to the emergency room because she was feeling lightheaded and dizzy. Fortunately, it was nothing serious. I remember visiting with the young doctor who was on call. The emergency room was rather quiet that evening, so we had ample time to talk. In the course of the conversation I asked him a question: "When you have a pain in a particular part of your body—say, you just banged your finger with a hammer—and you take pain medication, how does the medicine know to go to that part of the body?" His answer was, "It doesn't. The medication affects all parts of the body the same, you just sense relief in the area that was hurting the most."

Body of Christ—This week I talked to another lifelong friend who told me that after eighteen years of trying to conceive, he and his wife are expecting their first baby. They are elated, and so am I!

3. Members of the body are made to care for one another.

Physical body—The other day I felt a speck of dust in my eye. Immediately, another part of my body—my hand—went to the rescue, gently stretching my bottom eyelid and carefully removing the intrusive object. This happened quite naturally. No called staff meetings or strategy sessions took place between the eye and the hand; it was just a normal reflex action.

Body of Christ—This past week, a friend of mine broke off a relationship with his girlfriend. They had been dating for four years and had a genuine love for one another, but they felt that breaking up was the right thing to do. As soon as I heard about it, I called him to comfort him. It seemed to be a natural response.

4. Care for one another should be mutual.

Physical body—The apostle Paul discusses the interdependence of the physical body: "The eye cannot say to the hand, 'I don't need you.' And the head cannot say to the feet, 'I don't need you!'" (1 Corinthians 12:21). In the old days, we sang a song with these lyrics: "The knee bone connected to the thigh bone; the thigh bone connected to the hip bone; the hip bone connected to the back bone" and so forth. Cute song, but I don't think we understood the meaning of the lyrics. The truth is, there are "many parts, but one body" (v. 20), and they are all connected and dependent on each other.

Body of Christ—A wise pastor and friend once told me, "Don, there are three types of people in your church. Some are takers; they're always in need and if you let them, they'll drain you dry. Other relationships will be neutral; they don't demand a lot and they don't give much. Other people are givers; they will bless you, encourage you, and 'fill your cup.' Make sure that you maintain a good balance between the three types."

It was good advice. Ideally though, all three categories are flawed. The ideal model is *mutual care for one another*. The "takers" should learn how to give, the "neutrals" should learn to be proactive, and the "givers" must be sure that they too are receiving. There must be reciprocity, a mutual giving, in the body of Christ.

5. Care for one another should be equal.

Physical body—Paul also comments on the equality among the members of the physical body: "On the contrary, those parts of the body that seem to be weaker are indispensable, and the parts that we think are less honorable we treat with special honor" (1 Corinthians 12:22–23). Sure, some parts have a higher profile (for example, beautiful eyes usually get more comments than a person's liver), but all the parts are important and should be honored.

Body of Christ—Among the body of Christ, favoritism is strictly forbidden (James 2:9; 1 Timothy 5:21; Romans 2:11). Simply put, this means that we cannot pick and choose whom we will show care for. We should not show more care toward one person than we do another. Just as justice should be "blind," so should Care for One Another. Do we tend to comfort one of our children more than the others? Do we encourage one group of people but neglect others? Do we spend an inordinate amount of time with one couple but ignore other couples? The medicine of care should be dispensed equally.

6. Mutual care for one another is the key to unity.

Physical body—I recently read an article that promoted a threefold plan for physical well-being: eat right, exercise, and get plenty of sleep. Not surprisingly, if we will simply abide by these suggestions, we'll feel better physically and function more efficiently and effectively.

Body of Christ—What creates a deep, abiding sense of unity among believers? We often think that having the same theological beliefs is sufficient ("Are you a premillennialist? Great…so am I!") or that sharing political persuasions is key ("You voted for the Democratic candidate? Great…so did I!"), but through the years, I've known people who were theologically and politically aligned but fought like cats and dogs. To the contrary, I've known individuals who differed in their theological and political beliefs but enjoyed a genuine sense of oneness because they sincerely cared for each another. They were able to look beyond personal opinions, preferences, and beliefs and focus instead on issues of the heart. When showing concern for one another, we are focusing on universal, inherent issues.

Whenever a personal relationship is strained, the best prescription is to administer a generous dose of care for one another. When a church is fractured, the first step toward unity is for its members to express genuine care for one another.

Practical Ways to Care for One Another

1. Stay current with people's lives.

Consistently caring for others is difficult if you don't know what is going on in their lives. Keep in touch and visit regularly with people to discover the struggles and joys they are facing.

2. Concentrate on *doing* caring acts.

While care for someone may begin as an attitude, it must manifest itself in caring acts. Or, as the apostle Paul said, we need to *show it*: "I rejoice greatly in the Lord that at last you have renewed your concern for me. Indeed, you have been concerned, but you had no opportunity to *show it*" (Philippians 4:10; emphasis added).

Here are some suggestions on how to "put feet" to your care and concern:

Phone calls—Genuine care and concern can be communicated in a five-minute phone call. How many short calls can you make in one day—five? ten?

Written notes and letters—A few written sentences can convey care and concern. How long does it take to write a thoughtful card—five minutes? Could you write one or two per day?

Items of personal interest—I read of a salesman who made it a point to learn and remember the personal hobbies and interests of his clients. He subscribed to forty magazines, and every month he would scan the periodicals, looking for articles that would be of interest to his clients. He would then mail the article to the person along with a personal note. It was a great way to communicate, "I'm thinking about you."

3. Become interested in what other people are interested in.

The apostle Paul gave us the following command: "Each of you should look not only to your own interests, but also to the interests of others" (Philippians 2:4). This verse implies that: (1) We all have our own interests, (2) There's nothing wrong with considering our own interests, and (3) We should also think about the interest of others. Use your own interests as a cue to determine and consider the interest of others.

Consistently caring for others is difficult if you don't know what is going on in their lives. **Keep in touch and visit** regularly with people to *discover the struggles and joys they are facing.*

First, what are "interests"? Among other things, they are our needs (physical and emotional), desires, hopes, fears, and worries. Our interests are the areas we think about and are concerned about.

A good way to get into the habit of caring for others is to take the issues that concern us and use them as a reminder that other people probably have similar concerns. For instance, let's consider the following five areas on a personal level and then use them as a catalyst to consider the interests of others. In this exercise, think of a family member or friend whom you would like to care for. I'll use the name John as my friend.

- ***Needs***

     Physical—"I need to eat lunch today. I wonder where John is eating today."
     Emotional—"I'm hurting over some comments that were made in this morning's staff meeting. I wonder how John's day is going."

- *Desires*—"I would really like to travel to Europe. I wonder what John's favorite destination would be."
- *Hopes*—"I want to retire when I'm sixty. I wonder how John's retirement plans are going."
- *Fears*—"I'm afraid I'll get cancer someday. I wonder what fearful thoughts John struggles with."
- *Worries*—"I'm worried about my daughter who is away at college. I wonder if John is worried about his children in any way."

List some of your own personal interests and then use your list to prompt you to consider the interests of someone you care for.

My interests

Similar interest a loved one may have

_____   _____

_____   _____

_____   _____

4. Learn to enter into other people's "world."

We all live in at least three worlds simultaneously:
- *physical world* (we inhabit a place)
- *mental world* (our thoughts)
- *emotional world* (how we feel)

A good way to show care for someone is to enter into his or her world.

People feel cared for when we enter into their *physical world*.

"I pray that now at last by God's will the way may be opened for me *to come to you*. I long to see you so that I may impart to you some spiritual gift to make you strong—that is, that you and I may be mutually encouraged by each other's faith" (Romans 1:10–12; emphasis added).

People feel blessed when we take the time and effort to visit their place of work, their home, or their school and attend events that they are involved in. The first time I have lunch with a new friend, I insist on picking him up at his office because I want to enter into his physical world.

People feel cared for when we enter into their *mental world*.

"But, brothers, when we were torn away from you for a short time (in person, *not in thought*), out of our intense longing we made every effort to see you" (1 Thessalonians 2:17; emphasis added).

When I was a boy, my mother used to say to me, "Penny for your thoughts." It was her kind and gentle way to discover what I was thinking about. I felt so comfortable with her and was so assured of her caring response that I would share with her whatever I was thinking.

People feel cared for when we enter into their *emotional world*.

"Rejoice with those who rejoice; mourn with those who mourn" (Romans 12:15). This verse speaks of entering into another person's emotional state. When someone is sad, we should be sad. When he is happy, we should be happy.

To differentiate between entering someone's mental world and his emotional world, let's contrast two terms—sympathy and empathy. To *sympathize* with someone is to understand *mentally* what a person is going through: "I know you are disappointed." To *empathize* with someone is to identify *emotionally* with the feelings of another person to such an extent that you feel as she does: "I hurt that you are hurting. I feel sad inside that you are so disappointed."

5. Understand that caring for others will be a burden for us to bear.

"I face daily the pressure of my concern for all the churches. Who is weak, and I do not feel weak? Who is led into sin, and I do not inwardly burn? (2 Corinthians 11:28–29).

Caring for others will inevitably cause us sadness, disappointment, and hardship. It will cost us resources (finances, time, and energy), mental anguish, and emotional pain. Fortunately, we do not have to bear the burdens alone because God has told us we can cast them upon him (1 Peter 5:7), and he has told other believers to help us (Galatians 6:2). Nevertheless, we should anticipate the inconveniences, the dying to self, and the cost that caring for others will demand.

6. Look for unique and personal ways to express care for others.

I read of a man who purchased a top-of-the line Lexus. He picked up the car at the dealership and on his way home turned on the radio to try out the expensive stereo system. He happened to punch the first pre-set button and discovered that it was set to his favorite station. The second button was already set to his second most favorite station. He was amazed. A Lexus is a fancy car, but this was almost spooky. A quick call to the dealership solved the mystery. When he had turned in his former car as a trade-in, the service manager took the time to discover what stations the radio was tuned to and made the effort to program the man's new stereo. Quite a personal touch. Obviously, the dealership solidified a lifelong customer.

Several years ago, the University of Oklahoma and Florida State played for the national football championship. Thirty seconds after the game ended (Oklahoma won), I called a friend of mine who is an avid OU fan, just to congratulate him on his school's win. I wanted him to know I cared for him.

Everyone Needs Someone Who Cares

"No one is concerned for me. No one cares for my life" (Psalm 142:4).

The story is told about a man who went to the doctor after weeks of feeling bad. The doctor examined him carefully then called the patient's wife into his office. "Your husband is suffering from a rare form of anemia. Without treatment, he'll be dead in a few weeks. The good news is that it can be treated with proper nutrition."

The doctor then prescribed an unusual treatment that was likely to work: "You will need to get up early every morning and fix your husband a hot breakfast—pancakes, bacon and eggs, the works. He'll need a home-cooked lunch every day, and then an old-fashioned meat-and-potato dinner every evening. It would be especially helpful if you could bake frequently. Cakes, pies, homemade bread—these are the things that will allow your husband to live. And one more thing: His immune system is weak, so it's important that your home be kept spotless at all times. Do you have any questions?" The wife had none.

"Do you want to break the news, or shall I?" asked the doctor.

"I will," the wife replied.

She walked into the exam room. The husband, sensing the seriousness of his illness, asked her, "It's bad, isn't it?"

She nodded, tears welling up in her eyes.

"What's going to happen to me?" he asked.

With a sob, the wife blurted out, "The doctor says you're gonna die!"

This is a funny story (hopefully fiction), but it does put a contemporary spin on the same plight that the psalmist David suffered from when he wrote Psalm 142. At perhaps the lowest point in his life, while living in a cave, David felt like no one cared for him.

Have you ever felt that way? It is a hopeless feeling; a sense of being terribly alone in our pain and fear. A feeling of being disconnected and without help, cut off, overlooked, ignored, anonymous. It's a horrible feeling.

That's why the Bible instructs us to care for one another. No one should ever have to experience the pain of being alone.

Caring for Our Family

While we are to care for everyone we know, let me encourage you to prioritize your closest family members. Out of the six billion people on the face of the globe, who will care for Mary (my wife) and Sarah and Lauren (my two daughters)? Hopefully, many people, but for sure—I must.

It's amazing how much comfort we can feel and hope we can maintain if we know that at least one person in the world genuinely and deeply cares for us. Through the years, my wife and I have continually told our two daughters, "We love you so much. You are so special to us. I cannot imagine life without you. There's a place in my heart that belongs just to you. I will always love you and care for you. There's nothing that you can do to keep me from loving you. You can always come home to our house and be cared for. Even when you get married and have a family, our care will not cease and will extend to them as well. I think of you often during the day. I'm interested in your future. I care about your struggles, fears, dreams, and aspirations."

No one should ever have to experience the pain of being alone. No one in our immediate family should ever cry, *"No one cares for my life."*

Fortunately, there are other people who also care for Sarah and Lauren, but regardless of whether or not they will care for them tomorrow and the day after—Mary and I will.

I have communicated this same depth of care to Mary. Many times I have told her that I will always care for her and provide for her. As we get older, I have reassured her that if she becomes physically disabled or in need of constant medical attention—I will be there for her.

No one in our immediate family should ever cry, "No one cares for my life."

Name your immediate family members. Are they convinced of your abiding care for them?

Family member   **His or her level of confidence of your care**

_____

_____

_____

_____

Caring for Others

A nurse took the tired, anxious serviceman to the bedside. "Your son is here," she said to the old man. She had to repeat the words several times before the patient's eyes opened. Heavily sedated because of the pain of his heart attack, he dimly saw the young man in the Marine Corps uniform standing outside the oxygen tent. He reached out his hand. The Marine wrapped his toughened fingers around the old man's limp ones, squeezing a message of love and encouragement. The nurse brought a chair so that the Marine could sit alongside the bed. All through the night the young Marine sat in the poorly lit ward, holding the old man's hand and offering him words of love and strength. Occasionally, the nurse suggested that the Marine move away and rest awhile. He refused.

Whenever the nurse came into the ward, the Marine was oblivious of her and of the night noises of the hospital—the clanking of the oxygen tank, the laughter of the night staff members exchanging greetings, the cries and moans of the other patients. Now and then she heard him say a few gentle words. The dying man said nothing, only held tightly to his son all through the night.

At dawn, the old man died. The Marine placed the lifeless hand he had been holding on the bed and went to tell the nurse. While she did what she had to do, he waited. Finally, she returned. She started to offer words of sympathy, but the Marine interrupted her. "Who was that man?" he asked.

The nurse was startled. "He was your father," she answered.

"No, he wasn't," the Marine replied. "I never saw him before in my life."

"Then why didn't you say something when I took you to him?"

I knew right away there had been a mistake, but I also knew he needed his son, and his son just wasn't here. When I realized that he was too sick to tell whether or not I was his son, and I knew how much he needed me, I stayed."

Lord, give us the grace to care for one another.

Personal Journal

1. In your life, who has cared for you the most? What did he or she do to make you feel cared for?

_____

_____

2. Who in your life have you consistently and demonstrably cared for?

_____

3. Who is the most caring person you know? What does he or she do to show care for others?

_____

_____

4. Have you ever said to yourself, "No one cares for my life"?

_____

5. Write your own definition of Care for One Another.

_____

_____

6. On a scale from 1 to 10 (1 being, "I need to improve" and 10 being, "I do a good job"), how well do you do at caring for others?

    I rate myself a _____.

Group Time

Each member of the group should give his or her individual response to the first three questions. Allow about two minutes for each person's response. Allow all group members to share answers to question #1 before proceeding to question #2.

1. What was the most interesting concept in this chapter?
2. Share your responses to the first three Personal Journal entries.

As a group, process these discussion questions. These discussion questions have been prioritized. Depending on the time allowed for your group discussion, you may not be able to process all the questions.

a. In 1 Corinthians 9:9, the apostle Paul asks a rhetorical question: "Is it about oxen that God is concerned?" The obvious answer is no. Why do we often get so concerned about "oxen" even to the neglect of showing concern for human beings? What are some "oxen" that you tend to get obsessed with?

b. Near the end of his earthly ministry, Jesus had this conversation with Simon Peter, "Simon son of John, do you truly love me?...[then] Take care of my sheep" (John 21:16). How does this verse relate to the topic of caring for one another?

c. Discuss this statement: "The only way to serve Christ is to care for others."

d. Referring back to the section on using your own interest as a way to understand the interest of others, share some of the "personal interests" you have and then ask members of the group to share their areas of concern.

Chapter 7

CONFESS YOUR SINS TO ONE ANOTHER

"Confess your sins to each another" (James 5:16).

One day I received a call from a lady in our church who had just suffered a miscarriage. Miscarriages are a tremendous source of pain and grief. Several church members and I went to her house to *comfort* her and *pray with* her (two of the One Anothers). She was in deep anguish; she had been twelve weeks pregnant and had already decorated the baby's room. She wanted to show us the room, and just that morning she had created a framed collage in memory of the child.

As I sat there, listening to her grieve, I was able to enter into her sorrow. My empathy was so real that I began to cry for her.

Then a flood of memories went through my mind. I remembered that Mary and I had suffered three consecutive miscarriages early in our marriage. Back then, I didn't have the foggiest idea how to comfort someone. Instead of comforting Mary, I responded with logic and reasoning: "Sweetheart, a certain percentage of all pregnancies end in miscarriage; it's just a matter of statistics." I gave her a pep talk: "Mary, we'll get over this. Everything will be fine." And even tried to spiritualize the situation: "All things work together for good to those who love God." But I didn't offer what she needed—comfort. And when someone needs comfort but we give something else, we hurt that person further.

That day, sitting in the lady's den, I started to weep again. But this time it wasn't for the lady in that house; it was for the lady in my house—my wife. I had deeply hurt Mary years before but had never made it right.

That night, I told Mary about the visit and how God had spoken to me about my insensitivity toward her during those difficult times. I confessed my faults to her and asked her forgiveness. She was silent, and then she acknowledged that my reactions years ago had indeed hurt her. But she forgave me. I experienced the joy of Confess Your Sins to One Another and Mary shared with me the divine grace of Forgive One Another.

The need to confess our sins is obvious. We have all sinned (Romans 3:23) and to say that we have not is foolishness: "If we claim to be without sin, we deceive ourselves and the truth is not in us" (1 John 1:8). Most of us would never claim to be "without sin," yet our reluctance to confess is, in essence, the same thing. When we go year after year and never confess our wrongs to anyone, we are deceived and void of the truth.

[Note: In this chapter I'll focus on our need to confess to certain individuals, specific ways that we have wronged them. For example: "Cindy, I've been very critical of you lately and that's wrong." I also believe there is value in confessing our struggles and failures to others who have not necessarily been affected by them personally. For example: "Cindy, I'm really struggling with anger toward my kids."

> The issue is not, Have we sinned, but rather, What have we done about it?

Sharing our struggles (and sin) with others can be very therapeutic and often our friends, by offering prayer, counsel, and accountability, can help us overcome our struggles. But, in this chapter, I'll focus on our need to confess our sin to those whom we have offended.]

Most Christians acknowledge that we must confess our sins to God (1 John 1:9) and, they make it a regular part of their prayer life. But many of us neglect confessing to others when we sin against them.

Feeling Guilty

Hopefully, when we sin we will feel guilty. Feelings of guilt are the expected by-product of sin. When we do something wrong, we *should* feel guilty. Appropriate feelings of guilt are actually a sign of spiritual health. If we sin and *don't* feel guilt, something is wrong.

Testimony: The importance of feeling guilty when we have wronged someone

"To be honest, until recently, I'm not sure that I have felt a lot of guilt. My conscience just never bothered me. The Bible says the Holy Spirit will convict us of sin (John 16:8), but perhaps my heart was so hard or apathetic that he was unable to communicate to me. I just never felt guilty. But lately I've been asking God to sensitize my heart so that when I do offend him or someone else, it bothers me. Now there's a gentle tugging in my conscience that won't go away until I properly confess my wrong."

There are two dimensions to guilt—mental and emotional—and it's necessary to experience both. The mental aspect of guilt comes from cognitively acknowledging that I have done something wrong. (*The speed limit is 55, I'm going 70; therefore, I'm breaking the law. The Bible says to be gentle; I just spoke roughly to my children; that must have been wrong.*)

The emotional aspect of guilt comes as we realize that our sin is not only wrong, but that it has also *hurt* others and *hurt* God (the Bible says that we can grieve the Holy Spirit—Ephesians 4:30). This emotional response to our sin is called godly sorrow in the New Testament (2 Corinthians 7:10) and a contrite heart in the Old Testament (Psalm 51:17). According to 2 Corinthians 7:10, unless we enter into the emotions of how our sin has hurt others (that is, we experience godly sorrow), we probably will not change (in the Bible, repentance means to change).

Testimony: The importance of the emotional dimension of guilt

"For years I gave mental assent to the fact that I had wronged my wife by having selfish priorities. I had placed my career above our marriage. I knew that was wrong, and I would often ask her forgiveness; but I would inevitably hurt her again. At that point there was no emotional dimension to my guilt or my confession; it was just cerebral. I cognitively knew it was wrong and that I needed to confess. But one day I began to think about the emotional toll my sin had taken on my wife; I meditated on how deeply I had hurt her by my wrong priorities. At that point my feelings of guilt took the eighteen-inch plunge from my head to my heart. I began to feel sorrow for what I had done.

When I realized my sin had deeply hurt my wife, I became very sad. My sense of guilt reached a new dimension; I wasn't just giving mental assent to the fact that I had done wrong, I connected emotionally. I confessed again to God and to my wife, but this time the emotional dimension was there. 'Sweetheart, I realize now that my wrong priorities have hurt you deeply. I know it has caused you to feel neglected and at times unloved. I love you and don't ever want you to feel that way. Please forgive me.'

I can't say that I've not messed up again, but I do know that after that encounter I had a new and intense resolve not to do it again. I guess that's what the Bible means when it says godly sorrow will lead to repentance."

When was the last time you entered into the *emotionality* of how you have wronged someone? Did you experience godly sorrow?

_____

_____

Developing a Sensitive Conscience

God has given us a conscience through which he can speak to us when we have sinned. Our conscience is part of our spirit, so it can act independently of our minds. That's why our conscience can be bothered even though our minds may not register the offense.

God wants us to develop and maintain a sensitive conscience as opposed to one that is hardened and unresponsive (Romans 2:5; Hebrews 3:13). Our conscience remains pliable as we continually exercise the disciplines of confession and forgiveness.

Testimony: Developing a sensitive conscience

"One morning at work, I had a rather terse conversation with a fellow employee. At the time, I didn't think I had said anything wrong or offensive. But as soon as I left his office I had a nagging heaviness in my heart. Mentally I couldn't figure out what was going on, but I knew my spirit was troubled. I finally realized that my conscience was bothering me; I had offended my co-worker. I returned to his office and asked his forgiveness for my unkind words. I could tell by his reaction that I had indeed offended him. After I confessed my sin, the heaviness in my spirit lifted. I'm glad I listened to my conscience."

Inadequate Responses to Our Sin

It's important to understand what will *not* remove sin.

1. Time will not eradicate sin.

We often think that the more time that passes after we sin, the less influence our sin has and therefore our need to confess diminishes. *Yes, I hurt my wife. But that was twenty years ago, when we first got married.* Regardless of how much time has passed since we sinned, we still need to confess.

2. Our changed behavior does not eliminate our need to confess.

Yes, I hurt my children with my temper, but now I've changed. I don't have a bad temper any more. We rejoice in God's good work in your life, but you still need to confess.

Most Christians acknowledge that we must **confess** our sins to God (1 John 1:9) and they make it a regular part of their prayer life. **But many of us** neglect confessing to others when we sin against them.

3. Suffering the consequences of sin will not remove sin.

We may think that since we "paid our debt," our guilt is removed. *Yes, I sexually abused my daughter, but I spent five years in prison. I paid my debt to society.* Although you may have fulfilled society's requirements, you still must confess your sin to your daughter.

4. Our offender forgiving us does not eliminate our need to confess.

My husband is such a forgiving person. The other day I embarrassed him at a party and on the way home he forgave me—without me even asking. You are blessed to have a spouse who is quick to forgive, but his godliness is no excuse for your reluctance to confess.

Properly Dealing with Sin

When we sin against someone, there's only one proper thing to do—confess—to God and to whomever we offended.

To God—1 John 1:9: "If we confess our sins, he is faithful and just and will forgive us our sins and purify us from all unrighteousness."

To others—James 5:16: "Therefore confess your sins to each other and pray for each other so that you may be healed."

For instance, if you're married, how long has it been since these words came out of your mouth: *Honey, what I did to you was wrong. Would you forgive me?* If you have children, how long has it been since each child heard these words, *Sweetheart, I was wrong. Would you forgive me?* For some, the answer would be, "It's been a long time." For others the truth would be, "Never." Personally, I was forty-four years old when my father died, and in forty-four years I never heard him confess his sin to me; he never acknowledged the pain he had caused in our relationship.

When was the last time you confessed to a family member or friend?

_____

Write what you said.

_____

Confess Your *Own* Faults

Allow me to add a word to the first phrase of James 5:16. I realize I need to be careful here (Revelation 22:18), but I don't think it will violate the meaning of the phrase but rather enhance it. Here it goes…"Confess your *own* faults to one another" (added word in italics).

I do a lot of marriage counseling. Usually, in the fourth or fifth session I share the message of James 5:16 (confess your faults) and ask the couple to do just what the verse says, but invariably, most couples don't get it right. Instead of confessing their *own* sin, they begin confessing *their spouse's* sin. Obviously, this makes things worse; and indeed, it convolutes the essence of the verse.

We are never told to confess other people's sin; we are instructed to confess our own. Interestingly, this is often hard to do. When asked to consider the offenses that have taken place in my marriage, the first list that comes to my mind is how *I* have been violated, not how I have violated my wife. Jesus talked about this skewed perspective in Matthew 7:3: "Why do you look at the speck of sawdust in your brother's eye and pay no attention to the plank in your own eye?"

> How often should we confess? As often as we sin. But another safe answer is: more than we have and do.

But what about my spouse's (or, another person's) sin? If I'm not allowed to comment on it, who will? That's the Holy Spirit's job, not yours. "When he [the Holy Spirit] comes, he will convict the world of guilt in regard to sin" (John 16:8). From personal experience, I can testify that my wife doesn't respond very well when I try to convict her of her sin; but when the Holy Spirit speaks, she listens.

What If We Don't Confess Our Faults?

The admonition to confess our sins to God (1 John 1:9) is preceded and followed by a warning for those who refuse to admit their sin.

Verse 8: "If we claim to be without sin, we deceive ourselves and the truth is not in us."
Verse 9: "But if we confess our sins, he is faithful and just and will forgive us our sins."
Verse 10: "If we claim we have not sinned, we make him out to be a liar and his word has no place in our lives."

These are sobering words to anyone who will not admit the need to confess. The result of taking such a position is:
- We are self-deceived.
- We are void of the truth.

- We call God a liar.
- God's word has no place in our lives.

Not a pretty scenario.

I have never met anyone who claimed to be without sin. Only a few people in the world would deny that they have ever sinned. But I don't think these two verses were written just for this small group; they also apply to another group of people, perhaps to you and me. Follow my logic:

To say, "I do not sin" is similar to,

"I sin, but I don't see any need to confess it" which is similar to,

"I sin and I know I need to confess it but I don't."

In other words, practically speaking, there is not much difference between the person who claims to have no sin and the person who acknowledges his sin but refuses to confess it. Therefore, when we don't confess our sin we may suffer to some degree the four maladies listed in verses 8 and 10: We are self-deceived, we are void of the truth, we call God a liar, and God's word has no place in our lives

Confession Brings Healing

There is a wonderful by-product of confession—healing. Look again at 1 John 1:9 and James 5:16. John tells us that our confession to God will *purify* us; James says that our confession to others will bring *healing*. Not only is our guilt removed through confession, but relationships are healed.

Proverbs 28:13 underscores the tragedy of not confessing and the blessing of doing so: "He who conceals his sins does not prosper, but whoever confesses and renounces them finds mercy."

Indeed, confession is a prerequisite for spiritual and relational health, so let's learn how to speak a genuine confession.

Characteristics of a Good Confession

1. The scope of our confession should be equal to the scope of our offense.

When we sin, to whom should we confess? For instance, if we just *think* poorly about someone but don't actually say or do anything, do we still need to confess to that person?

The scope of our confession should be equal to the scope of our offense.

If we do not openly offend a person, then we don't need to confess to him or her. But since God always knows our sin and he is offended by it, we always need to confess to him.

For instance, if I'm in the car with my spouse and two kids and speak unwholesome words to my spouse (a violation of Ephesians 4:29), I should confess to God, to my spouse, and to my children, since they were all in the scope of the offense. If my sin adversely affects a large group of people (an office staff, a church), I should confess to the group. All sin offends God, so we must always confess to him (1 John 1:9). When our sin offends others we must confess to them as well (James 5:16).

2. Confessions are most effective if we take the initiative to confess without having to be confronted by those we offend.

For instance, can you sense the difference in these two scenarios?

Joan: Hey Bob, got a minute?

Bob: Sure, what's up?

Joan: When we were having lunch yesterday you said something that really offended me.

Bob: Oh yeah? I'm sorry. What did I say?

Joan: It was the comment about my work on the Meyers project.

Bob: Oh, that. Yeah, that probably did come across a little tacky. Would you forgive me?

Bob: Hi Joan, got a minute?

Joan: Sure, what's up?

Bob: Yesterday, when we had lunch together, I made a tacky comment about your work on the Meyers project. The truth is, you've done a great job. It was wrong of me to say what I did. Would you forgive me?

If we initiate the conversation without having to be confronted by the person we offended, our confession is more meaningful.

3. Enter into the emotions of how you have hurt the other person.

For instance, if we yell at our children, we are not only *wrong*, but we have hurt our children as well. We must deal with both the technical aspect of being wrong and the emotional hurt.

That's why a good confession will often involve comforting words: *I'm so sorry that I hurt you by yelling at you.* This emotion is called "godly sorrow" (2 Corinthians 7:10). As mentioned earlier in this chapter, according to this verse, this sorrow for our sin is the only thing that will lead us to true repentance, that is, change: "Godly sorrow brings repentance."

4. Be specific. Name the sin.

Hurts don't come in generalities; they are specific. So our confession must be specific. Can you sense the difference between these two statements?

Honey, if I've ever done anything to offend you, would you forgive me?

Honey, God has convicted me that I have had a critical spirit toward you. For instance, last night I criticized you about the hotel arrangements you made for our vacation. I should have been grateful that you took the initiative to plan such a nice trip.

> Sin is not only wrong, but it also *hurts* those we offend. A genuine confession should attempt to enter into the pain we have

A good confession should mention the specific wrong (*I was insensitive, critical, unsupportive*) and even include examples.

5. Use the phrase "I was wrong" instead of "I'm sorry".

The phrase "I'm sorry" implies little, if any, personal responsibility. It can have several subtle meanings that can actually negate any admittance of being wrong:

- *I'm sorry what I said offended you (but it wouldn't have offended you if you weren't so hypersensitive).*
- *I'm sorry you feel neglected (but after all, you are overly dependent).*
- *I'm sorry you were upset at the party (but no one else seemed to be).*

However, the phrase "I was wrong" acknowledges personal responsibility.

6. After saying, "I was wrong," refrain from saying anything else.

Often, after we confess, we are tempted to:

- Minimize the offense—*Yeah, I got mad, but that's not the main issue.*
- Rationalize/justify—*The reason I got mad was...*
- Blame others—*I wouldn't have become angry if you hadn't...*
- Offer a trite confession—*Okay, okay; I'm sorry.*
- Ignore the offense—*Let's talk about something else.*
- Confess in order to avoid further conflict or embarrassment—*Our company is coming soon; let's get this behind us.*

Any attempt to rationalize, justify, or blame will dilute our confession. Even though what we're tempted to say may be true, it is inappropriate and counterproductive to discuss these issues at the same time we are confessing.

Of these six "substitutes" for confession, which do you most often struggle with?

_____

Why are you often reluctant to speak a genuine confession?

_____

Hurts don't come in generalities; they are specific. So our confession *must be specific.*

7. Ask forgiveness.

For a confession to be complete, we should ask for the person's forgiveness. The best way to do this is simply to ask, "Will you forgive me?" If you have genuinely and properly confessed and have exhibited a degree of godly sorrow over your actions, the ball has now been served into the offended party's court. It is now his decision whether or not to forgive you, but you should be free from guilt whether he does or doesn't. Even if he refuses to forgive you, you have done everything you can do to right the wrong and you should be released from feelings of guilt. In certain situations, particularly involving legal systems, restitution may still need to be paid (a fine for a speeding ticket, a jail sentence for a crime committed), but we should no longer be debilitated by feelings of guilt.

8. To be thorough in our confession, we should minister to the hurt we caused the other person(s).

In addition to admitting our wrong and asking forgiveness, it is appropriate and even advantageous to *comfort* those we have offended. This involves admitting that we not only *wronged* them, but that we also *hurt* them. Words of comfort may sound like this: *I know that when I criticized you it really hurt you. I feel sad about that. It really grieves me that I hurt you.*

Questions and Answers Regarding Confessing Our Sins to One Another

Having taught for many years on the topic of confessing our sins to one another, I've noticed some reoccurring questions regarding the topic. I'll address these issues in a Q&A format.

Q - I have a real problem with impatience. It seems like every other day I offend my wife or children. I've confessed to them a million times. Do I need to keep confessing every time I offend them with my impatience? Sometimes I get tired of confessing, and I even think they get weary of hearing it again.

A - Yes. Every time we wrong someone we need to confess, even though the same offense is often repeated. Otherwise, the hurt and guilt will accumulate. Also, our constant confessing will hold us accountable to continue to pray for genuine and permanent change.

The Bible speaks of spiritual strongholds (2 Corinthians 10:4)—specific sins that have a tremendous hold over us and ones that we have difficulty controlling. What sin *that affects other people* do you struggle with the most? [For instance, being critical, impatient, harsh, angry, selfish, neglectful, hurtful with words.] _____

Have you ever confessed this sin to others? Are you reluctant to continue confessing this sin, simply because you've confessed it so many times before? _____

Q - Recently, I was in a situation in which someone else wronged me. In the midst of discussing the matter, I said something to him I shouldn't have. My perspective on this is that his offense was a hundred-dollar event, and mine was a five-dollar event. He has not yet confessed to me his "big" offense, so I'm reluctant to confess my "small" offense. It just seems unfair for me to have to confess first.

A - I'm not sure what "value" the two events had, but let's just assume your estimation is correct—perhaps what you did wrong was small compared to what was done to you. Regardless, you need to confess your wrong. The fact that you were wronged does not justify your wrong, and the fact that some issues are major and some minor has nothing to do with whether or not they should be confessed. Confessing "small" sins will keep us accountable to be careful about how we react to those who have offended us.

Write about a time when this "big sin, little sin" scenario happened to you. Did you properly deal with your wrong?

_____

_____

Q - Years ago, when our children were at home, I had a big problem with my temper. My outbursts of anger were quite regular. I'm grateful to say that God did a deep work in my life in that area. I confessed my sin to God and my wife and have received forgiveness from both. And I have really changed. The last time my daughter visited us, she even commented on how different I am. My question is—now that I've changed—do I still need to confess to my children that my outbursts of anger were wrong?

A - Yes, you need to confess to your children (and anyone else you might have offended by your temper). The fact that you have changed does not negate the fact that you sinned against your children nor does it remove their hurt. Even the fact that they see how God has worked in your life and that they're able to rejoice with you doesn't eliminate the need to confess to them. You must not only deal with the _wrongness_ of your actions (by confession), but you also need to deal with the _hurt_ that you caused your children.

It will be important for you not to allow your children to minimize what happened (_Dad, it's no big deal; that was a long time ago. Dad, don't worry about it; I can see how much you've changed._) Help them get in touch with the hurt that they might have felt (_When I yelled at you in anger, you must have felt...belittled, betrayed, embarrassed, confused. I'm so sorry I hurt you like that._)

As God continues to work on areas of sin in our lives, his work is not complete until we both change _and_ properly deal with the hurt our sin has caused others.

Write about a particular sin that you used to struggle with but have now, at least to some degree, have under control. Have you properly dealt with how this sin hurt people in the past?

_____

_____

Q - The Lord has convicted me about a way in which I offended my spouse twenty-five years ago. I have confessed it to God and received his forgiveness. Do I need to confess it to my spouse?

A - It's good that you have heard from the Lord, and it is good that you have confessed your sin to him. But that's not enough. Your sin hurt two people—God and your spouse—and you need to confess to both. Also, the fact that it happened twenty-five years ago does not negate your need to confess.

Q - I have recently felt guilt over some rebellious years I had as a teenager, but both of my parents are deceased. What can I do?

A - Sometimes, we are convicted of and/or bothered by a past event, but we're not able to respond to the offended person, as we would like.

- We were rebellious toward a parent who is now deceased.
- We had an abortion.
- We violated someone and he or she refuses to talk to us.

If it is impossible to contact the person we offended, the following steps will help bring relief from guilt:

- Share with God your sorrow and confess to him.
- At an appropriate time and place, share with a friend your sorrow and grief. Allow him or her to comfort you.

One day while passing a house of ill fame, Socrates, the famous Greek thinker, noticed one of his students inside. Stepping to the doorway, Socrates called out to his disciple. The latter hid himself, as Adam did when he committed the first sin. However, the youth eventually had to come before his mentor, his face crimson with shame. He hung his head, expecting a stern rebuke from his teacher. But Socrates spoke in the tones of a true father: "Come forth, my son, I pray you, come forth! To leave this house is not disgraceful; the only disgraceful thing was to have entered it."[1]

When we have sinned, the best thing to do is to "come forth." We need to confess. But instead of confessing our sins, we are usually tempted to justify ourselves, rationalize our actions, or blame others. The only way to remove our guilt and bring healing to relationships is to confess.

No doubt, it is hard to do. The words, "I was wrong. Would you forgive me?" don't naturally spill from our lips. But we must learn to say them.

Personal Journal

1. Write about a time in your life when someone confessed that he had wronged you and then asked your forgiveness.

_____

_____

2. Emotionally and relationally, who is your closest family member? When was the last time you confessed to this individual a specific way in which you have hurt him or her?

_____

3. When you were a child, did your parents ever confess their sins to you? _____

If you are a parent, have you ever confessed your sins to your children? _____

4. Think of the people whom you are relationally close to. If you're married, include your spouse, and if you have children, include them. As you consider each person, process through the following list.

      a. Alone, ask God to convict you of ways you have wronged this person.

      b. Meditate on the fact that what you did was not just technically wrong, but that it also hurt this person. Allow God to sorrow your heart over your offense.

      c. Ask God to forgive you (1 John 4:9).

      d. At an appropriate time and place, share with this person your sorrow over hurting him, confess to him, and ask his forgiveness (James 5:16).

5. As you reflect back on your life, allow the Holy Spirit to convict you of offenses you might have committed years earlier that have never been properly resolved (For instance, _I unjustly fired an employee in anger. I stole money from my employer. I neglected my children when they were young._) As you consider each incident, process through the four points listed in #4.

6. Write your own definition of Confess Your Sins to One Another.

_____

_____

7. On a scale of 1 to 10 (1 being, "I need to greatly improve" and 10 being, "I do a good job"), how well do you confess your sins to others?

      I rate myself a _____.

Group Time

Each member of the group should give his or her individual response to the first two questions. Allow about two minutes for each person's response. Allow all group members to share answers to question #1 before proceeding to question #2.

1. What was the most interesting concept in this chapter?
2. Share your responses to the first three Personal Journal questions.

As a group, process these discussion questions. The discussion questions have been prioritized. Depending on the time allotted for your group discussion, you may not be able to process all the questions.

a. Read Matthew 7:3–5. What can we learn from the "log-and-splinter" illustration?
b. The Greek word for confess is *homologeo,* which literally means "to speak the same thing" (*homos,* same, *lego,* to speak). How does this meaning relate to our confession of sin?
c. Read Mark 1:5, and Acts 19:18 and discuss these situations in which there was an open acknowledgement of sin.
d. Read 2 Samuel 12:13. Although in this chapter we've not talked about confessing our sins to a "spiritual mentor," briefly discuss the advantages of doing so.

BE DEVOTED TO ONE ANOTHER

"Be devoted to one another" (Romans 12:10).

Soon after Jack Benny died, George Burns was interviewed on TV. "Jack and I had a wonderful friendship for nearly fifty-five years," Burns said. "Jack never walked out on me when I sang a song, and I never walked out on him when he played the violin. We laughed together, we played together, we worked together, and we ate together. I suppose that for many of those years we talked every single day."

In a sweet and sincere way, George Burns and Jack Benny were devoted to one another.

The Greek word for "devotion" is *philostorgos*, which means "to cherish one's kindred, to be fond of, to be fraternal toward fellow Christians, tenderly loving, and tenderly affectionate." Devotion implies a deep level of commitment. It is perhaps, the only One Another which we can, in some measure, ration out.

Through the years, I have sensed that I have developed a deep sense of devotion to certain individuals, but not to everyone. For instance, my highest devotion is to my wife and children; that is expected. But even among my friends, I am more devoted to some than others. This may smack of favoritism, but my conscience doesn't bother me in the least.

It seems as if the Lord also had those to whom he was deeply devoted: the twelve disciples. Even among the twelve there were three whom he seemed to confide in the most (Peter, James, and John), and some would even suggest that he was closest to John. He didn't love them any more than the others, but he did feel called to spend more time with them, and he allowed them to know him in ways the others didn't. The three were invited to be with Christ on the Mount of Transfiguration, which was perhaps the highlight of his earthly ministry, and in the Garden of Gethsemane, which was arguably the lowest point in his earthly ministry.

Devotion implies a deep level of commitment. It is perhaps, the only One Another which we can, in some measure, *ration out.*

So in the course of life, we'll sense a natural yearning to be devoted to certain people. In my thirty years of ministry I have served on the staff of several large churches. If I totaled their combined membership, it would be in the tens of thousands. I don't feel strongly obliged to maintain a close relationship with all of the members, but there are some for whom I would drop what I'm doing and respond to their needs in a moment's notice. I am devoted to them.

The Meaning of Being Devoted to Someone
Devotion implies several different things:

1. Value—*I highly value you; you are important to me.*

Devotion implies value, worth, and importance. It's does not have a "take-it-or-leave-it" attitude. Devotion does not say, "If you were to be taken from me, I'd be just fine," but rather, "You are such an important part of my life; I can't imagine going through life without you."

2. Commitment—*I am committed to you. I pledge to be lovingly involved in your life.*

Years ago, I developed a deep friendship with seven men in my church. Our odyssey began when we went on a mission trip together. On the trip we had a visitation from God that supernaturally knit our hearts together. Through the years we continued to meet and minister together.

Several years later the Lord moved my family and me to a different city. Several months after moving, I became clinically depressed. I was almost incapacitated. I had a hard time getting out of bed in the mornings and the simplest of tasks seemed overwhelming.

I called one of my friends and confided in him how bad I was feeling. He comforted me over the telephone and prayed for me. He asked if he could share my burden with the other guys; I said, "Sure." About forty-five minutes later he called me back and said, "Brother Don, I've called all the guys and we're coming to see you. We're going to get in a van at three o'clock in the morning, drive to your house (a four-hour trip), pray for you, and then head back to town and go to work."

I was deeply touched. These are busy men—an engineer at Boeing, a graphic artist, a businessman—and yet with forty-five minutes' notice they all arranged to take the time to go and pray for Brother Don.

These men were, and are, devoted to me, and I am profoundly moved by their love.

3. Long-term commitment—*I'm in this relationship for the long haul. I'll walk with you through the good times and the bad. We are friends for life.*

A college student walked into a photography studio with a framed picture of his girlfriend. He wanted the picture duplicated. This involved removing it from the frame. In doing this, the studio owner noticed the inscription on the back of the photograph: "My dearest Tom, I love you with all my heart. I love you more and more each day. I will love you forever and ever. I am yours for all eternity." It was signed "Diane," and it contained a final P.S.: "If we ever break up, I want this picture back."

When we are devoted to someone, there can be no P.S.

I have some friends to whom I have said, "We're friends for life. I'll say the prayer at your funeral or you'll say the prayer at mine. Even if you move to another country, our friendship will remain."

Who are some of your long-term friends? _____

_____

4. Priority—*My life, like yours, is multifaceted. But I want you to know that you are a priority to me. I will always prioritize our relationship. When necessary, you will be the sole focus of my attention.*

If someone asked me, "Among all your friends and family members, who was the one person most devoted to you?" My answer would be, my mother. As I write this chapter, listing these characteristics of devotion, Mom personifies each one. I was a priority in her life.

I have two daughters in college, so I am well aware of the financial commitment it takes to finance a college education. In the midst of my own sacrificial giving, I have been reflecting on the fact that Mom and Dad helped finance my college education. Although I didn't notice back when I was in school, it now occurs to me that Mom and Dad didn't take vacations during my college years and that they drove the same old beat-up car for many years. When it came time to pay the bills, my college tuition was always on the top of the stack; other demands and desires had to wait.

When we are devoted to someone, her life will take precedence over other things.

5. Meeting needs—*I am aware of your physical and emotional needs and want to be a part of meeting those needs.*

A sense of devotion is an attitude, a mind-set, a state of the heart, but it will inevitably manifest itself in practical ways. In particular, when I am devoted to someone I will be concerned about his needs and delight in helping to meet his needs.

I will strive to meet the physical needs (food, rest, shelter, security, finances), emotional needs (encouragement, support, comfort), and spiritual needs (peace, joy, assurance) of the one to whom I am devoted.

6. Faithfulness—*Relationally, I'm going to bind myself to you. I hope my deep commitment will make you feel secure.*

Out of the furnaces of war come many true stories of sacrificial friendship. One such story tells of two friends in World War I who were inseparable. They enlisted together, trained together, were shipped overseas together, and fought side by side in the trenches. During an attack, one of the men was critically wounded in a field filled with barbed-wire obstacles, and he was unable to crawl back to his foxhole. The entire area was under a withering enemy crossfire, and it was suicidal to try to reach him. Yet his friend decided to try. Before he could get out of his own trench, his sergeant yanked him back and ordered him not to go. "It's too late. You can't do him any good, and you'll only get yourself killed."

> A sense of devotion is an attitude, a mind-set, a state of the heart, but it will inevitable manifest itself in practical ways.

A few minutes later, the officer turned his back, and instantly the man was gone after his friend. A few minutes later, he staggered back, mortally wounded, with his friend, now dead, in his arms. The sergeant was both angry and deeply moved. "What a waste," he blurted out. "He's dead, and you're dying. It just wasn't worth it."

With almost his last breath, the dying man replied, "Oh, yes, it was, Sarge. When I got to him, the only thing he said was, 'I knew you'd come, Jim!'"

Relational security comes from knowing my friend will be consistently faithful to me to the end.

7. Vulnerable communication—*I am willing to share with you the deep issues of my life and you can trust me with the deep concerns of your life. I want to know you in a deep, intimate way.*

For a relationship to deepen, there must be vulnerable communication. We must get below surface issues and talk about issues of the heart: struggles, fears, doubts, aspirations, dreams, and frustrations. While I may not feel the freedom to share these deep thoughts with just anyone, I do sense that I am safe in sharing them with those to whom I am devoted.

I have a friend at church to whom I am devoted. We've been working on our relationship for about four years. I see him at church several times a week, and we meet about once a month for a cup of coffee and private conversation. The last time we met he shared with me some struggles he was having with a few Old Testament passages, such as, *Did God really ask Abraham to sacrifice his son? That's barbaric!* And, *I really can't understand why a loving God would order the Israelites to ravage and destroy the inhabitants of the Promised Land; those people were there first!* These are issues most of us have struggled with but have usually been reluctant to voice.

But on this particular day my friend did share them. I'm not sure what he expected me to say, but I just nodded my head and said, "Tom, you're right, some of those things are just really hard to understand." At the end of our time together he thanked me for listening; he also said he had never felt the freedom to share those thoughts with anyone else.

I'm devoted to Tom. I'm there for the long term. There's nothing he could share with me that would alter our friendship. And the more deeply we share with one another, the more steadfast our relationship becomes.

8. Tenderness—*You are very dear to me.*

There's a beautiful passage in 1 Thessalonians in which the apostle Paul discloses his tender sentiments toward his friends. Read carefully: "As apostles of Christ we could have been a burden to you, but we were gently among you, like a mother caring for her little children. We loved you so much that we were delighted to share with you not only the gospel of God but our lives as well, because you had become so dear to us" (1 Thessalonians 2:7–8).

When thinking about those to whom I am devoted, a phrase that often comes to my mind is, "You are very dear to me." There is a tender affection, a softness, a warmth toward these friends. There is a looking beyond their faults and feeling a deep tenderness and love.

I'm not a grandfather yet—my daughters are not married—but in the past several years I have sensed in my heart a grandfatherly love for some of the children at the church. I buy them gifts when I'm on vacation and take them to the museum on Saturdays. The best word to describe my feelings for these children is the word *dear*. They have become dear to me. And that, I believe, is a part of what it means to be devoted to someone.

9. Consistency—*You can count on me to be a consistent source of love and care.*

Around our house we have two dogs and one cat. One of our dogs, named Tal, is consistently loving toward Madeleine, the cat. He's always gentle and patient. Our other dog, named Chloe, is quite different. For several months at a time she will also be loving and patient with Madeleine; but then, for no obvious reason, she'll snap at Madeleine and chase her as if to kill her. It's not surprising that Madeleine prefers to spend time with Tal; Chloe is just too unpredictable. She never knows on any particular day whether Chloe will be loving or aggressive. After a while, the erratic behavior is just not worth tolerating.

When thinking about those to whom I am devoted, a phrase that often comes to my mind is, *"You are very dear to me."*

On a human level, we all have friendships like that. One moment your acquaintance is loving; the next moment he's after you.

I realize that consistent love is something to which we all must aspire to give in *all* of our relationships, but in order to communicate a deep sense of devotion to someone, this particular aspect of love is essential. The claim of "I am devoted to you" is severely weakened by inconsistency.

Evaluate your own level of consistency among your close friends.

_____

_____

10. Love, even unto death—*I would die for you.*

A little boy was told by his doctor that he could save his sister's life by giving her some blood. The six-year-old girl was near death, a victim of a disease from which the boy had made a marvelous recovery two years earlier. Her only chance for restoration was a blood transfusion from someone who had previously conquered the illness. Since the two children had the same rare blood type, the boy was the ideal donor.

"Johnny, would you like to give your blood for Mary?" the doctor asked. The boy hesitated. His lower lip started to tremble. Then he smiled, and said, "Sure, Doc. I'll give my blood for my sister."

Soon the two children were wheeled into the operating room—Mary, pale and thin; Johnny, robust and the picture of health. Neither spoke, but when their eyes met, Johnny grinned.

As his blood siphoned into Mary's veins, one could almost see new life come into her tired body. The ordeal was almost over when Johnny's brave little voice broke the silence: "Say, Doc, when do I die?"

It was only then that the doctor realized what the moment of hesitation, the trembling of the lip, had meant earlier. Little Johnny actually thought that in giving his blood to his sister he was giving up his life! And in that brief moment, he had made his great decision.

When we are truly devoted to someone, her life is more valuable than our own. Jesus emphasized this deep level of love when he said, "Greater love has no one than this, that one lay down his life for his friends" (John 15:13).

In a magazine cartoon, a thief was wearing a "Lone Ranger" mask. His gun was pointed toward his frightened victim as he yelled: "Okay, gimme all your valuables!"

The victim began stuffing into the sack all his *friends*.

The most precious possessions I have in life are those friends to whom I am devoted and who are devoted to me. Without them, life would be very empty.

Personal Journal

1. Name some of your long-term friends. Do they sense that you are devoted to them?

_____

2. In your life, who has demonstrated that they are devoted to you?

_____

3. Name some of the people you would like to be devoted to.

_____

4. Write your own definition of Be Devoted to One Another.

_____

_____

5. On a scale from 1 to 10 (1 being "I need to improve" and 10 being, "I do a good job"), how well do you do at being devoted to for others?

   I rate myself a _____.

Group Time

Each member of the group should give his or her individual response to the first two questions. Allow about two minutes for each person's response. Allow all group members to share answers to question #1 before proceeding to question #2.

1. What was the most interesting concept in this chapter?
2. Share your responses to the first three Personal Journal questions.

As a group, process these discussion questions. The discussion questions have been prioritized. Depending on the time allotted for your group discussion, you may not be able to discuss all the questions.

a. Read Hebrews 13:5 and discuss the fact that Christ is devoted to us.
b. In Philippians 2:19–24 and 1 Corinthians 4:17, read about the apostle Paul's relationship with a young man named Timothy. In 2 Timothy 4:10 read about his relationship with a man named Demus. Talk about the contrast between the two relationships.

SERVE ONE ANOTHER

"Serve one another in love" (Galatians 5:13).

In the late 1800s, a large group of European pastors came to one of D. L. Moody's Northfield Bible Conferences in Massachusetts. Following the European custom of the time, each guest put his shoes outside his room to be cleaned by the hall servants overnight. But of course this was America, and there were no hall servants.

Walking the dormitory halls that night, Moody saw the shoes and determined not to embarrass his brothers. He mentioned the need to some ministerial students who were there, but he was met only with silence or pious excuses. Moody returned to the dorm, gathered up the shoes, and, alone in his room, the world's most famous evangelist began to clean and polish the shoes. Only the unexpected arrival of a friend in the midst of the work revealed the secret.

When the foreign visitors opened their doors the next morning, their shoes were shined. They never knew by whom. Moody told no one, but his friend told a few people, and during the rest of the conference, different men volunteered to shine the shoes in secret. Perhaps the episode is a vital insight into why God used D. L. Moody as he did. Moody was a man with a servant's heart, and that was the basis of his true greatness.

Galatians 5:13 sets forth a simple but profound directive: "Serve one another." Here's the complete verse: "You, my brothers, were called to be free. But do not use your freedom to indulge the sinful nature, rather, serve one another in love." Notice that the primary focus of this verse, and indeed the entire chapter, is on freedom. The first verse of chapter 5 reads, "It is for freedom that Christ has set us free."

So what is the connection between freedom and our call to Serve One Another? An interesting anecdote might help explain.

A friend of mine was speaking to the twelve-hundred-member student body of a charismatic Bible school. The chapel service began with forty-five minutes of high-energy, intense, genuine worship, so by the time he got up to speak, the place was wired.

My friend took advantage of the students' unabashed enthusiasm to introduce his topic in a rather dramatic way. He excitedly greeted the students: "I have good news for you today! We have been set free!" The students responded with high-spirited whoops. He continued, "Where the spirit of the Lord is—there is freedom!" The students became even more excited. Then he asked a simple question: "Yes, we've been set free, *but set free to do what?*" The audience was silent.

This dramatic introduction focused on an important truth: We have been set free so that we can *serve and love others*.

For a moment, don't worry about what we've been set free from, or even the process of being set free. These are critical issues, but if we get enamored with them, we may "miss the forest for the trees." Regardless of from what you have been set free, to what degree you have been set free, and even how you have been set free, the issue is: What are you going to do with your freedom?

> We have been set free so that we can serve one another in love.

If we're not careful, as Christians, we may sit happily and snugly—sometimes smugly—in our born-again condition and never grasp "the rest of the story." Yes, we are to rejoice in the fact that we have been set free, but we must press on and ask ourselves the same question that my friend asked the students: "Why?"

The answer is simple but profound: We have been set free so that we can serve one another in love.

Indeed, the apostle John even says that if we don't have love for one another, it may be an indication that the truth is not in us (1 John 4:20-21). And the apostle Paul makes it clear that freedom is merely a means to an end (Galatians 5:13).

List some things from which Christ has set you free and then consider the fact that you have been set free in order to serve others.

_____

_____

The Character of a Servant

James Packard shares these insights into what it means to serve one another:
"Servant" in our English New Testament usually represents the Greek word *doulos* (bond slave). Sometimes it means *diakonos* (deacon or minister); this is strictly accurate, for *doulos* and *diakonos* are synonyms. Both words denote a man who is not at his own disposal but is his master's purchased property. Bought to serve his master's needs, to be at his beck and call every moment, the slave's sole business is to do as he is told. Christian service therefore means, first and foremost, living out a slave relationship to one's Savior (1 Corinthians 6:19–20).

What work does Christ set his servants to do? The way that they serve him, he tells them, is by becoming the slaves of their fellow servants and being willing to do literally anything, however costly, irksome, or undignified, in order to help them. This is what love means, as he himself showed at the Last Supper when he played the slave's part and washed the disciples' feet.

When the New Testament speaks of ministering to the saints, it means not primarily preaching to them but devoting time, trouble, and substance to giving them all the practical help possible. The essence of Christian service is loyalty to the king expressing itself in care for his servants (Matthew 25:31–46).

Only the Holy Spirit can create in us the kind of love toward our Savior that will overflow in imaginative sympathy and practical helpfulness toward his people. Unless the Spirit is training us in love, we are not fit persons to go to college or a training class to learn the know-how or particular branches of Christian work. Gifted leaders who are self-centered and loveless are a blight to the church rather than a blessing.

Made to Serve

The Dead Sea is so named because it contains no fish or plant life. It has such a high concentration of salt and minerals that nothing can live in its waters. What accounts for this unusual condition? There are no outlets! A great volume of water pours into the sea, but nothing flows out.

Many of us suffer from the same problem in the spiritual realm. Our spiritual lives become stagnant because, although we have received abundantly from the river of the Lord's goodness, we have not shared his goodness with others. We hoard what we have received from God. If this continues, in time, we may discover that even our receiving is restricted: "You do not have, because you do not ask God. When you ask, you do not receive, because you ask with wrong motives, that you may spend what you get on your pleasures" (James 4:2–3).

It is the Lord's intent that we be channels of his goodness. "As I have loved you, so you must love one another" (John 13:34).

The great violinist Niccolo Paganini willed his marvelous violin to the city of Genoa on the condition that it must never be played. The wood of such a fine instrument, while used and handled, wears only slightly; but set aside, it begins to decay. Paganini's lovely violin has today become worm-eaten and useless except as a relic. Likewise, a Christian's unwillingness to serve may soon destroy his capacity for usefulness.

Consider again the illustration of the Dead Sea and apply it to your life. Do you have tangible "outlets" through which God's grace and goodness can flow through you to other people? If so, what are some of these outlets?

_____

_____

Spirit-Empowered Service

As with all of the One Anothers, motive and empowerment are important. *Why* do we do what we do and *by what power* do we operate?

In Richard Foster's book *Celebration of Discipline,* he differentiates between self-righteous service and true service. Author Paul Robbins summarizes Foster's thoughts in the following sentences:

Self-focused service is concerned with impressive gains. It enjoys serving when the service is titanic or growing in that direction.
Christ-focused service doesn't distinguish between small and large. It indiscriminately welcomes all opportunities to serve.

Self-focused service requires external reward, appreciation, and applause.
Christ-focused service rests content in being hidden. The divine nod of approval is sufficient.

Self-focused service is highly concerned about results. It becomes disillusioned when results fall below expectations.
Christ-focused service is free of the need to calculate results; it delights only in service.

Self-focused service is affected by feelings.
Christ-focused service ministers simply and faithfully because there is a need. The service disciplines the feelings.

Self-focused service insists on meeting the need; it demands the opportunity to help.
Christ-focused service listens with tenderness and patience. It can serve by waiting in silence.

A Powerful Testimony of Serving Others

While serving as a missionary in India, Doug Nichols had a surprise, divine encounter that illustrates the dramatic effect that our serving others can have. Here, in his own words, is this powerful story:

While serving with Operation Mobilization in India in 1967, I spent several months in a TB sanitarium with tuberculosis. Even as a patient, I tried to give tracts to the patients, doctors, and nurses, but no one would take them. You could tell that they weren't really happy with me, a rich American (to them all Americans were rich), being in a government sanitarium. They didn't know that serving with O.M., I was just as broke as they were.

I was quite discouraged with being sick, having everyone angry at me, not being able to witness because of the language barrier, and no one even bothering to take a tract or Gospel of John. The first few nights, I would wake around 2:00 A.M. coughing. One morning as I was going through my coughing spell, I noticed one of the older (and certainly sicker) patients across the aisle trying to get out of bed. He would sit up on the edge of the bed and try to stand, but because of weakness would fall back into bed. I really didn't understand what was happening or what he was trying to do. He finally fell back into bed exhausted. I then heard him begin to cry softly.

The next morning I realized what the man was trying to do. He was simply trying to get up and walk to the bathroom. Because of his sickness and extreme weakness he was not able to do this, and being so ill he simply went to the toilet in the bed.

The next morning the stench in our ward was awful. Most of the other patients yelled insults at the man because of the smell. The nurses were extremely agitated and angry because they had to clean up the mess, and moved him roughly from side to side to take care of the problem. One of the nurses in her anger even slapped him. The man, terribly embarrassed, just curled up into a ball and wept.

The next night, also around 2:00 A.M., I again awoke coughing. I noticed the man across the aisle sit up to again try to make his way to the washroom. However, still being so weak, he fell back whimpering as the night before. I'm just like most of you. I don't like bad smells. I didn't want to become involved. I was sick myself but before I realized what had happened, not knowing why I did it, I got out of my bed and went over to the old man. He was still crying and did not hear me approach. As I reached down and touched his shoulder, his eyes opened with a fearful questioning look. I simply smiled, put my arm under his head and neck, and my other arm under his legs, picked him up.

Even though I was sick and weak, I was certainly stronger than he was. He was extremely light because of his old age and advanced TB. I walked down the hall to the washroom, which was really just a smelly, filthy small room with a hole in the floor. I stood behind him with my arms under his arms, holding him so he could take care of himself. After he finished, I picked him up and carried him back to his bed. As I began to lay him down, with my head next to his, he kissed me on the cheek, smiled, and said something, which I suppose, was "thank you."

It was amazing what happened the next morning. One of the other patients whom I didn't know woke me around 4:00 with a steaming cup of delicious Indian tea. He then made motions with his hands (he knew no English) indicating he wanted a tract. As the sun came up, some of the other patients began to approach, motioning that they would also like one of the booklets I had tried to distribute before. Throughout the day people came to me, asking for the Gospel booklets. This included the nurses, the hospital interns, the doctors, until everybody in the hospital had a tract, booklet, or Gospel of John. Over the next few days, several indicated they trusted Christ as Savior as a result of reading the Good News!

What did it take to reach these people with the Good News of salvation in Christ? It certainly wasn't health. It definitely wasn't the ability to speak or to give an intellectually moving discourse. Health, and the ability to communicate sensitively to other cultures and peoples are all very important, but what did God use to open their hearts to the Gospel? I simply took an old man to the bathroom. Anyone could have done that.

Of all the One Anothers, perhaps Serve One Another best characterizes the essence of Christian ministry. Indeed, when the apostle Paul referred to his ministry among the churches, he used the word *service*. "Now, however, I am on my way to Jerusalem in the service of the saints there. Pray that I may be rescued from the unbelievers in Judea and that my service in Jerusalem may be acceptable" (Romans 15:25, 31).

Interestingly, in the culture of the New Testament period, slaves were a large part of the population. Many slaves were well-educated men; many were capable of managing large estates and the business interests of their owners. Neither Jesus nor Paul ever criticized the institution of slavery. Although Paul stated that in Christ there is neither bond nor free, all are alike (1 Corinthians 12:13; Galatians 3:28), he also encouraged slaves to be content in the condition in which they were "called" (1 Corinthians 7:20–23), and he urged masters to treat their slaves fairly and justly (Ephesians 6:9).

Because servants were such a prevailing part of the society, it must have shocked the first-century church when Paul instructed the early church to Serve One Another. I can just imagine Paul teaching this message in someone's home, the servant having just served the meal. Perhaps Paul, pointing to the servant's actions, would say, "Yeah, just like that. Serve one another just like this servant has been serving us."

Of course, Paul was just reiterating the attitude clearly taught by Christ and modeled throughout his earthly ministry. Imagine the shocking impact this statement must have had on Jesus' followers: "The Son of Man did not come to be served, but to serve" (Matthew 20:28). That was a unique recruitment slogan: "Hey guys, come be like me. I have become a servant!"

Indeed, we are called to be servants.

Practical Ways to Serve One Another

1. Be attentive to the needs of others.

I have a personal fetish about employees of service organizations who neglect their customers. Several years ago, my wife and I went to a restaurant to eat a late lunch. It was about three in the afternoon, so the lunch crowd was gone; we were the only people in the restaurant. After being seated by the hostess, we sat for about ten minutes before receiving any type of service. I counted ten waitpersons in the restaurant. Many were talking to each other, some were setting the tables for the dinner crowd, but no one saw to our needs. I soon became irritated at the lack of attention and asked to talk to the manager. In a kind way, I said, "The purpose for which your restaurant exists is to serve its patrons. Your waitstaff is so busy doing other things that they are neglecting the very reason you exist—customers!"

I experienced the same lack of attention and focus upon deboarding a plane at the Detroit airport. Most airlines are conscientious enough to provide several service agents who stand at the gate when incoming flights are deboarding. They are there to give connection information to travelers who have a connecting flight to catch. On this particular day, there were two agents, armed with computer printouts with gate information; but to my surprise, they were talking and laughing with each other, totally ignoring the passengers. Several passengers were waiting for information, but the gate agents were oblivious to their needs. I finally interrupted their conversation and asked for information. They looked at me as if I had offended them by interrupting their conversation. I didn't have time to ask for the manager, but if I had, I would have kindly shared, "The purpose for which your airline exists is to serve its patrons. Your gate agents are so busy talking among themselves that they are neglecting the very reason you exist—customers!

I've given two illustrations regarding what good service *is not* like; let me share a positive experience. My wife and I have a favorite restaurant in Dallas—the Four Seasons. And whenever we go, we ask for a particular waiter named José. José is pleasant, friendly, and *very attentive*. His job is to serve and he does it well. In an inconspicuous way he always keeps one eye focused on our table. When the water glass gets half-empty, he fills it to the brim. He anticipates our need for more butter; he is concerned as to how our main course is prepared. In general, he realizes that the focus of the evening is not about him and his needs; it's about his customers.

Around the McMinn house, we have a cute little saying that comes in handy when we want to focus on a particular individual—"It's all about *you*." It helps us to focus on the main thing. For instance, when we're celebrating Sarah's birthday, we say, "Sarah, it's all about *you*. What do *you* want to do today? Where do *you* want to eat dinner? What movie do *you* want to see?" When it's Lauren's turn, we say to her, "It's all about *you*."

When we Serve One Another, it's all about others—their needs, desires, and preferences. It's not about us; it's all about them.

2. Be willing to perform menial, mundane tasks.

When we have a deep desire to serve others, we will even delight in doing menial and mundane tasks—routine and commonplace jobs that would normally be outside of our scope of interest and responsibility. We'll be willing to house-sit, run errands, wash dishes, do yard work, or move furniture—simply because we want to serve and help others.

Years ago I accepted the position of associate pastor at a large church that was located in a different city than we were currently living in. The senior pastor is one of the premier preachers in America; he is in constant demand both as a speaker and advisor. The week before our furniture arrived we painted the inside of our new house. On the first night of our painting project I was surprised to see the pastor show up in his old clothes, grab a brush, and begin to paint. One of the most sought-after preachers in America was painting my house. More than helping to paint our house, he was serving us, and I felt blessed and loved.

3. Serve others cheerfully.

We are often reluctant to serve others, but the Bible speaks of being *eager to serve* (1 Peter 5:2), serving *wholeheartedly* (Ephesians 6:7), and serving *with gladness* (Psalm 100:2).

Archbishop Secker used to say, "God has three sorts of servants in the world: Some are slaves, and serve him from fear; others are hirelings, and serve for wages; and the last are sons, who serve because they love."

We will discover that servanthood is indeed the good life. Here is a story about the losing and finding of life in a person.

When we have a deep desire to serve others, we will even delight in doing menial and mundane tasks—*routine and commonplace jobs* that would **normally be outside of our scope** of interest and responsibility.

Marian Preminger was born in Hungary in 1913 and lived in a castle with her aristocratic family, surrounded with maids, tutors, governesses, butlers, and chauffeurs. Her grandmother, who lived with them, insisted that whenever they traveled, they take their own linens, for she believed it was beneath their dignity to sleep between sheets used by common people.

While attending school in Vienna, Marian met a handsome young Viennese doctor. They fell in love, eloped, and married when she was only eighteen. The marriage lasted only a year, and she returned to Vienna to begin her life as an actress.

While auditioning for a play, she met the brilliant young German director, Otto Preminger. They fell in love and soon married. They went to America soon thereafter, where he began his career as a movie director. Unfortunately and tragically, Hollywood is a place of dramatic illustrations of people "biting, devouring, and consuming" one another. Marian was caught up in the glamour, lights, and superficial excitement and soon began to live a sordid life. When Preminger discovered it, he divorced her.

Marian returned to Europe to live the life of a socialite in Paris. In 1948 she learned through the newspaper that Albert Schweitzer, the man she had read about as a little girl, was making one of his periodic visits to Europe and was staying at Gunsbach. She phoned his secretary and was given an appointment to see Dr. Schweitzer the next day. When Marian arrived in Gunsbach she discovered he was in the village church playing the organ. She listened and turned pages of music for him. After a visit he invited her to have dinner at his house. By the end of the day she knew she had discovered what she had been looking for all her life. She was with Dr. Schweitzer every day thereafter during his visit, and when he returned to Africa he invited her to come to Lambarene and work in the hospital.

Marian did—and she found herself. There in Lambarene, the girl who was born in a castle and raised like a princess, who was accustomed to being waited on with all the luxuries of a spoiled life, became a servant. She changed bandages, bathed babies, fed lepers—and became free. Marian titled her autobiography *All I Ever Wanted Was Everything*. She could not get the "everything" that would satisfy and give meaning until she could give everything. When she died in 1979, the *New York Times* carried her obituary, which included this statement from her: "Albert Schweitzer said there are two classes of people in this world—the helpers, and the nonhelpers. I'm a helper."

Personal Journal

1. Who, in your life, has best demonstrated a servant's heart toward you? What did this person do to serve you and others?

_____

2. Write about the last time you served someone.

_____

3. Read and meditate on Matthew 20:25–28 and write down your reflections on these verses.

_____

_____

4. Think of a way in which you could serve someone this coming week and write it down.

_____

5. Write your own definition of Serve One Another.

_____

_____

6. On a scale from 1 to 10 (1 being "I need to improve" and 10 being, "I do a good job"), how well do you do at serving others?

       I rate myself a _____.

Group Time

Each member of the group should give his or her individual response to the first two questions. Allow about two minutes for each person's response. Allow all group members to share answers to question #1 before proceeding to question #2.

1. What was the most interesting concept in this chapter?
2. Share your responses to the first three Personal Journal questions.

As a group, process these discussion questions. The discussion questions have been prioritized. Depending on the time allotted for your group discussion, you may not be able to discuss all the questions.

a. As a group, discuss this statement, "The only way to serve Christ is to serve one another."

b. As a group, discuss this statement by James Packer, "When the New Testament speaks of ministering to the saints, it means not primarily preaching to them but devoting time, trouble, and substance to giving them all the practical help possible."

c. Earlier in this chapter, we discussed the fact that Christ has set us free so that we might serve others. Read 1 Peter 4:10 and discuss God's purpose in giving us spiritual gifts. Have each group member share what his or her spiritual gifts are and how the gifts could be used to serve others.

d. Read Ephesians 6:7 and discuss what the verse teaches about servanthood.

e. What would be the antithesis of having a servant's heart?

BE KIND TO ONE ANOTHER
"Be kind . . . to one another" (Ephesians 4:32).

As Gandhi stepped aboard a train one day, one of his shoes slipped off and landed on the track. He was unable to retrieve it as the train had already begun to move. To the amazement of his companions, Gandhi calmly took off his other shoe and threw it back along the track to land close to the first. Asked by a fellow passenger why he did so, Gandhi smiled. "The poor man who finds the shoe lying on the track," he replied, "will now have a pair he can use."

One of the highest compliments we can receive is for someone to say about us, "He is a kind person."

Imitating God

"You are kind, O Lord" (Psalm 86:5).

One of the attributes of God is that he is kind. Yes, he is holy, just, sovereign, and righteous, but he is also kind. When we are kind to others, we are emulating God.

It was God's kindness that prompted him to redeem us: "When the kindness and love of God our Savior appeared, he saved us" (Titus 3:4). And it is his kindness that draws us to him: "Do you show contempt for the riches of his kindness, tolerance and patience, not realizing that God's kindness leads you toward repentance?" (Romans 2:4).

So if we are to be "imitators of God" (Ephesians 5:1), we must be kind. Otherwise, we misrepresent him.

Unfortunately, that's not always the case. I've been in the ministry for thirty years. It saddens me to say that some of the most tacky, unkind people I have ever known were Christians. I once served on staff with a man who was just downright mean-spirited. What was really sad was that he seemed to think that the Christian truths he embraced and his high level of morality justified, even compelled, his behavior.

It is possible to be correct but not kind, to be orthodox but lack grace, and even to be truthful but hurtful at the same time. But while it is possible, it is not right. God's people must be kind. If we are not, I doubt that we have been touched deeply by His Spirit, for kindness is a fruit of being filled with the Holy Spirit (Galatians 5:22). Indeed, it should be a constant factor in our lives. "Always try to be kind to each other and to everyone else" (1 Thessalonians 5:15).

And our acts of kindness should come from pure motives. Or, as Romans 12:9 says, "Love must be sincere." Consider the young man in a Boy Scout uniform who helped a nun across the street. He was very solicitous, guiding her carefully through traffic and giving a smart salute when they got to the other side. "Thank you very much, young man," said the nun. "Oh, that's all right," said the scout. "Any friend of Batman is a friend of mine!"

The "Personality" of Be Kind to One Another

Kindness is an attribute that is better *caught* than *taught*. So listed below are some characteristics of a kind person and some anecdotes and real-life examples of what these traits look like in everyday life.

1. Be gracious, cordial, polite, and courteous; don't be rough, rude, coarse, crude, or blunt.

"The Lord is gracious" (Psalm 111:4).

There should be a sense of grace and finesse about our behavior. We should always be polite and courteous.

Even difficult situations can be handled with poise. The story is told of an insurance sales manager who was known for his tact and diplomacy. One of his young salesmen was performing so poorly that he had to be terminated. The manager called him in and said, "Son, I don't know how we're ever going to get along without you, but starting Monday we're going to try."

2. Be thoughtful, considerate, helpful, unselfish, and solicitous; don't be thoughtless, inconsiderate, insensitive, or self-absorbed.

"For I know your eagerness to help, and I have been boasting about it to the Macedonians" (2 Corinthians 9:2).

> One of the highest compliments we can receive is for someone to say about us, "He is a kind person."

Have you heard of the Pierre de Coubertin International Fair Play Trophy? Many people regard it as the highest honor in sports. The trophy is named for the founder of the modern Olympic games, and it has been awarded annually for the past twenty-eight years to people in sports who have demonstrated nobility of spirit. It is big news in Europe, but it has not been given much recognition in the United States.

In the past, the trophy has gone to a Hungarian tennis player who pleaded with officials to give his opponent more time to recover from a cramp and to a high school basketball coach who forfeited the Georgia (U.S.) state championship after he found out that one of his players was scholastically ineligible. The first trophy went to an Italian bobsledder named Eugenio Monti for a gesture that exhibited a touch of class. In the two-man bobsled event at the 1964 Innsbruck Olympics, Monti was the leader after his final run. The only one given a chance to beat him was Tony Nash of Great Britain. As Nash and his teammate got ready for their final run, they discovered that a critical bolt on their sled had snapped at the last moment. Monti was informed of the problem and immediately took the corresponding bolt from his own sled and sent it up to Nash. Nash fixed his sled and came hurtling down the course to set a record and win the gold medal. Several years ago it was awarded to Danish paddlers who were competing in the marathon tandem kayak-racing event at the world championships in Copenhagen. Danish paddlers were leading when their rudder was damaged in a portage. British paddlers, who were in second place, stopped to help the Danes fix it. The Danes went on to defeat the British by one second in an event that lasted nearly three hours.

Stories like these –acts of thoughtfulness and unselfishness-should occur frequently in the body of Christ because we are taught to Be Kind to One Another.

3. Be understanding and sympathetic; don't be callous or hard-hearted.

"Be sympathetic" (1 Peter 3:8)

A tombstone cutter was busily engaged in his shop when his friend dropped in for a visit. The friend, while looking about the shop, noticed a headstone that had been there for several years. The inscription had been cut on it, but the words were useless, for the stone had been in storage all that time. Curious, the friend asked why. "The people who ordered it were not able to pay for it," came the laconic reply. "And it stays here until they bring the money." "But what good is it doing you here?" the friend asked. "No good! No good at all!" replied the cutter with some anger. "Well, then," continued his friend, "if those folks haven't been able to pay for it yet—it must have been years—your chances of collecting are pretty slim. Did it ever occur to you that you might place that stone where it belongs? At least it will be doing some good. It just takes up valuable room here." "That's poor business!" was the curt comment of the stonecutter. "It's never poor business to be kind to people and to go out of your way to help people who are in trouble." Having said this, the friend walked out of the shop and was on his way.

> There should be a sense of grace and finesse about our behavior. We should always be polite and courteous.

A month passed before he returned to that shop. He looked around the room. The stone was gone. "Well, I see you got rid of that stone," he commented. "Did they pay you for it?" "No!" replied the stonecutter. "But I placed the stone where it belongs anyhow." "That's poor business!" reminded his friend, mockingly. "I know it is," replied the stonecutter. "But after your last visit here, my conscience started to torment me about it. I got to putting myself in that family's place, for I know that they haven't had the money to pay for it. Every time I came into this shop, that white stone haunted me like a ghost until finally I took it out and put it where it really belongs. Then, afterward, when I found out how happy it made the family, I lost my head completely." "How?" "Well, yesterday when they came in here to pay me for the stone, I refused the money. That's how foolish I'm getting to be." "Foolish? I wonder…" replied his friend.

4. Be patient, tolerant, and long-suffering; don't be impatient, edgy, or easily annoyed.

"Be patient with everyone" (1 Thessalonians 5:14).

James Hewitt tells this story about the kindness of a father toward his son. "We have some friends who have a little boy who was born with a severe handicap that would cause him to go into very violent seizures without any warning. The father would usually be the one holding the boy during worship services. On one particular occasion when the little guy started into a seizure, the father got up and with a strong yet gentle love carried the boy to the back of the sanctuary where he held him close to his chest and rocked him, whispered to him, and did all he could to help his son through. One thing I noticed most of all was that there was no hint of embarrassment or frustration in the father's face—only love for his hurting son. I felt God speak to my own heart and in so many words say, 'That's just the way I love you through your imperfections. I'm not embarrassed to have people know that you are my son.' That's love!"

5. Be generous, charitable, benevolent, and big-hearted; don't be stingy, miserly, sparing, or begrudging.

"Be generous and willing to share" (1 Timothy 6:18).

Shortly after World War II came to a close, Europe began picking up the pieces. Much of the Old Country had been ravaged by war and was in ruins. Perhaps the saddest sight of all was that of little orphaned children starving in the streets of those war-torn cities. Early one chilly morning an American soldier was making his way back to the barracks in London. As he turned the corner in his jeep, he spotted a little lad with his nose pressed to the window of a pastry shop. Inside, the cook was kneading dough for a fresh batch of doughnuts. The hungry boy stared in silence, watching the cook's every move.

The soldier pulled his jeep to the curb, stopped, got out, and walked quietly over to where the little fellow was standing. Through the steamed-up window he could see the mouth-watering morsels as they were being pulled from the oven, piping hot. The boy salivated and released a slight groan as he watched the cook place them onto the glass-enclosed counter ever so carefully.

The soldier's heart went out to the nameless orphan as he stood beside him. "Son, would you like some of those?" The boy was startled. "Oh, yeah—I would!" The American stepped inside and bought a dozen, put them in a bag, and walked back to where the lad was standing in the foggy cold of the London morning. He smiled, held out the bag, and said simply: "Here you are." As he turned to walk away, he felt a tug on his coat. He looked back and heard the child ask quietly, "Mister, are you God?" We are never more like God than when we are kind.

6. Be compassionate and merciful; don't be uncaring, unconcerned, or callous.

"Be compassionate" (1 Peter 3:8).

In Booker T. Washington's autobiography, *Up from Slavery*, Mr. Washington recalled a beautiful incident of an older brother's love. He said the shirts worn on his plantation by the slaves were made of a rough, bristly, inexpensive flax fiber. As a young boy, the garment was so abrasive to his tender, sensitive skin that it caused him a great deal of pain and discomfort. His older brother, moved by his brother's suffering, would wear Booker's new shirts until they were broken in and smoother to the touch. Booker said it was one of the most striking acts of kindness he had experienced among his fellow slaves.

7. Be forgiving, tolerant, lenient, and forbearing; don't be exacting, demanding revenge, or unforgiving.

"Forgive whatever grievances you may have against one another" (Colossians 3:13).

When William Ewart Gladstone was Chancellor of the Exchequer, he sent down to the Treasury for certain statistics upon which to base his budget proposals. The statistician made a mistake. But Gladstone was so sure of this man's accuracy that he did not take time to verify his figures. He went before the House of Commons and made his speech based on the incorrect figures that had been given him. His speech was no sooner published than the newspaper exposed its glaring inaccuracies.

Mr. Gladstone was naturally overwhelmed with embarrassment. He went to his office and sent at once for the statistician who was responsible for his humiliating situation. The man came full of fear and shame, certain that he was going to lose his position. But instead,

Gladstone said: "I know how much you must be disturbed over what has happened, and I have sent for you to put you at your ease. For a long time you have been engaged in handling the intricacies of the national accounts, and this is the first mistake that you have made. I want to congratulate you, and express to you my keen appreciation."

8. Be gentle and sympathetic; don't be rough, challenging, difficult, or harsh.
"Be completely gentle" (Ephesians 4:2).

When Wesley visited Rathby to preach in the church, as he ascended the pulpit a child sat on the steps directly in the way. Instead of asking, "Why is that child allowed to sit there?" he gently took the child in his arms, kissed her, and then placed her on the same spot where she had been sitting.

When I was a child, I brought a toy pellet gun to church one Wednesday evening. A friend and I found an empty room next to the fellowship hall, lined up some paper cups, and had target practice. One of the pastors of the church unexpectedly came into the room, and we knew we were in trouble. But instead of the expected reprimand, he said, "Hi boys. Looks like you're having fun. Boy, that's a neat pistol you've got. Can I shoot it?" Our tenseness eased as he shot several pellets at the targets. But I'll never forget what came next. He bent over, picked up the pellets off of the floor (the ones he had shot), and handed them to me. His graciousness and kindness made a deep and lasting impact on my young heart.

9. Be careful with your speech; don't be tacky, careless, or hurtful with your words.
"Let your conversation be always full of grace, seasoned with salt" (Colossians 4:6).

The Bible has a lot to say about our speech:
- It is powerful (James 3:3-8).
- It should be consistently wholesome (James 3:9-12).
- What we say and how we say it usually gives an accurate picture of what we're like on the inside (Matthew 12:34).
- It is the "litmus test" of our religious testimony (James 1:26).

While it is often true that kind actions speak louder than well-meaning words, it is also true that hurtful and mean-spirited words speak louder than alleged but insincere kindness.

If we are to Be Kind to One Another, we must be careful what we say. Every word out of our mouths must first be filtered (*Is what I'm about to say necessary, timely and edifying?*) and then seasoned with grace (*What is the most graceful way that I can say what I want to say?*).

In a country church of a small village an altar boy serving the priest at Sunday mass accidentally dropped the cruet of wine. The village priest struck the altar boy sharply on the cheek and in a gruff voice shouted: "Leave the altar and don't come back!" That boy became Titto, the Communist leader. In the cathedral of a large city an altar boy serving the bishop at Sunday Mass accidentally dropped the cruet of wine. With a warm twinkle in his eyes the bishop gently whispered: "Someday you will be a priest." That boy grew up to become Archbishop Fulton Sheen.

While it is often true that kind actions speak louder than well-meaning words, *it is also true* that hurtful and mean-spirited words speak louder **than alleged but insincere kindness.**

---

10. Be diplomatic, tactful, prudent, and discreet; don't be oppositional, domineering, forceful, or overassertive.

"Show true humility toward all men" (Titus 3:2).

British statesman and financier Cecil Rhodes, whose fortune was used to endow the world-famous Rhodes Scholarships, was a stickler for correct dress—but apparently not at the expense of someone else's feelings. A young man invited to dine with Rhodes arrived by train and had to go directly to Rhodes's home in his travel-stained clothes. Once there he was appalled to find the other guests already assembled, wearing full evening dress. After what seemed a long time Rhodes appeared, in a shabby old blue suit. Later the young man learned that his host had been dressed in evening clothes but put on the old suit when he heard of his young guest's dilemma.

Practical Ways to Be Kind to One Another

While I was working on this chapter I shared a short devotional on the topic with some members of my church and then asked them to write down some practical ways to Be Kind to One Another. Here are some of their responses:

Put other people's feelings before your own; say nice words; be available; be considerate of feelings, beliefs and desires; don't be crabby—be sweet-spirited; think of other people's needs first; share a smile with someone; let your body language be gracious; be a good listener; treat others with respect; be gentle; show that you care; have a sweet disposition; show concern; be genuine; be understanding; give people attention; anticipate people's needs; be polite; do something nice; prioritize other people; be helpful; be friendly; give with no expectation of receiving in return; take people seriously; show respect.

There's little ambiguity or mystery to this particular One Another. It's really quite simple and obvious. It reminds me of a restaurant in Manhattan that is named *Eat Here—Now*. There's no question as to the purpose of the proprietor; the name is a clear, straightforward indication of what goes on inside the building.

In like manner, the Bible says, "Be kind." There's not much vagueness in that statement. It's not an obscure or archaic concept. We know what to do; we just need to do it.

Personal Journal

1. Who is the kindest person you have ever known? What did he or she *do* that expressed kindness?

_____

_____

2. What is the kindest thing that anyone has ever done for you?

_____

_____

3. If asked to describe you, would those who know you well portray you as a kind person? What are some of your "rough edges" that need to be sanded down in order for you to be more kind?

_____

_____

4. Write your own definition of Be Kind to One Another.

_____

_____

5. On a scale from 1 to 10 (1 being, "I need to improve" and 10 being, "I do a good job"), how well do you do at Be Kind to One Another?

       I rate myself a _____.

Group Time

Each member of the group should give his or her individual response to the first two questions. Allow about two minutes for each person's response. Allow all group members to share answers to question #1 before proceeding to question #2.

1. What was the most interesting concept in this chapter?
2. Share your responses to the first three Personal Journal questions.

As a group, process these discussion questions. The discussion questions have been prioritized. Depending on the time allotted for your group discussion, you may not be able to discuss all the questions.

a. Discuss this statement: "There is never any excuse for being unkind."

b. Read Proverbs 19:17 and Matthew 25:40 and discuss what these passages teach.

c. Read Titus 3:4 and Ephesians 2:6–7 and discuss the fact that Jesus Christ was the ultimate expression of God's kindness toward us.

d. Read Acts 14:17 and discuss the *practical* aspect of God's kindness toward us. How can we express kindness to others in practical ways?

SPUR ONE ANOTHER ON TOWARD LOVE AND GOOD DEEDS

"And let us consider how we may spur one another on toward love and good deeds"
(Hebrews 10:24).

During the administration of Calvin Coolidge, an overnight guest at the White House had a particularly embarrassing experience. At breakfast he was seated next to the President when he noticed Coolidge take his cup of coffee, pour a large amount into the saucer, and slowly put in a lot of cream and sugar.

The guest immediately followed suit. In some haste he also poured some coffee into his saucer. Then came his embarrassment, when he saw the President take his own saucer filled with the coffee and place it on the floor for the cat.

Influence. All of us wield some degree of it. People are watching us; some are following our example.

This particular One Another is particularly intriguing because it provides for the perpetuation of the other One Anothers.

Notice that there are two directives in this verse:

1. *Spur one another on toward love and good deeds.* This means that we are not only responsible for *doing* the One Anothers, but we are also responsible for *encouraging others* to do the One Anothers.
2. *Consider how.* This means that we need to think about, strategize on, meditate on, and plan to do the first directive.

A Mandate for Parents

Hebrews 10:24 should be the mantra of every Christian parent: Before my child leaves my house, I want her to know *how* to minister all thirty-five of the One Anothers and be *motivated by gratitude* to live her life loving others.

This creates an interesting approach to childhood development. Perhaps this takes some of the mystique out of Proverbs 22:6: "Train a child in the way he should go." It doesn't say, "Discipline a child when he deviates from the way in which he should go" but rather instructs us to take a positive, proactive approach. Can you imagine the mental, emotional, and spiritual health of a child who has learned how to prefer, accept, comfort, and encourage others, along with the other One Anothers?

A Mandate for Spiritual Leaders

Although Hebrews 10:24 is a directive to all believers, it certainly applies to those of us who are in positions of spiritual leadership. I've been an ordained minister for thirty years. Unfortunately, for many of those years I had no clue as to what my "job" was. I now believe that my primary job description is Hebrews 10:24. I am to be the "Chief One-Another Giver" in my church. My job? To give, model, facilitate, affirm, and teach the one Anothers.

As a pastor, perhaps my primary calling is to fulfill this verse—to spur my church members on toward love and good deeds. Perhaps this is the essence of the call of Ephesians 4:11–12: "He gave some to be apostles, and some to be prophets, and some to be evangelists, and some to be pastors and teachers, *to prepare God's people for works of service*" (emphasis added). How do I "prepare God's people for works of service"? I teach them how to love.

Practical Ways to Spur One Another On

1. Give to others.

One of the basic principles regarding the distribution of the One Anothers is that it is difficult, if not impossible, to give something that we have not first received. If I have never been comforted, it will be difficult for me to comfort others. If I do not sense that I have been accepted, I'll be reticent to accept others. So one of the best ways for us to spur others on toward love and good deeds is simply to share *with* them love and good deeds.

I enjoy taking people out to eat and picking up the tab. Recently, my family and I took another couple out for lunch following the Sunday morning service to celebrate a birthday. Right before we left the church to go to the restaurant, my daughter, Lauren, asked if several of her college friends could join us. Of course, I said yes.

> This particular One Another is particularly intriguing because it provides for the perpetuation of the other One Anothers.

About halfway through the meal, I flagged down the waiter, gave him my credit card, and asked him to charge everyone's meal to my account. When it was time to leave, everyone was very grateful and appreciative of my gesture.

On the way home, Lauren thanked me for treating her friends to lunch and then asked me an interesting question: "Why did you do that?" My initial response was simply that I enjoy treating people to a nice meal; it gives me joy to give. But then I searched a little deeper and the Lord took me back to an incident that happened to me thirty years earlier.

When I was a college student attending the University of Texas at Austin, two friends of mine and I decided to take a trip to Acapulco during spring break. It was cheaper to fly out of Houston so we drove there and stayed there over the weekend. At the time, I was serving as minister of music at a small church in Austin, so I suggested that we attend worship services at First Baptist Church of Houston, which, at that time was a flagship church in our denomination. Gerald Ray was the minister of music, and he was an icon among ministers of music.

After the service, I approached Gerald, introduced myself, and told him I was a fellow minister of music. He greeted me warmly, showed interest in me, and then, to my surprise, invited me to lunch. I told him that I had two traveling companions, and he invited them to come along as well.

I remember going to a cafeteria and sitting with Gerald, his family, and another couple from his church. And then I'll never forget what happened. When it came time to pay the bill; Gerald had already paid for our meals.

I grew up poor so this was a big deal to me, and the impact went far beyond the fact that it saved me a few dollars. I was stunned that this man, having never met me before, would be so hospitable (Show Hospitality to One Another), gracious (Be Kind to One Another), and generous…both to my friends and to me.

Now fast-forward thirty years. I believe that one reason I enjoy treating people to a nice meal is that Gerald Ray once treated me to a nice meal. Gerald *gave* to me in a way that impacted my life, and in so doing he "spurred me on toward love and good deeds."

Write about a time in your life when someone *gave* one of the One Anothers to you (encouragement, comfort, support, etc.) and their giving caused you to want to give to someone else.

_____

_____

2. Model a giving lifestyle.

Several months after I treated Lauren's friends to lunch, on a Saturday night, Lauren announced that on the following day she was having Sunday lunch with a few orchestra members (at the time she was the director). When I asked her who was going to pay, she replied, "I am; I want to treat them to lunch."

Lauren is by nature very giving and gracious, but I wonder if she might have been "spurred on" to this act of love by seeing it modeled in her father's life. Love and good deeds are better caught than taught.

Edgar Guest has written a poignant poem entitled *I'd Rather See a Sermon* that speaks to the importance of modeling:

> I'd rather see a sermon than hear one any day.
> I'd rather one should walk with me than merely show the way.
> The eye's a better pupil and more willing than the ear;
> Fine counsel is confusing, but example always clear.
> And the best of all the preachers are the men who live their creeds,
> For to see the good in action is what everybody needs.
> I can soon learn how to do it if you'll let me see it done,
> I can watch your hands in action, but your tongue too fast may run.
> And the lectures you deliver may be wise and true;
> But I'd rather get my lesson by observing what you do.
> For I may misunderstand you and the high advice you give,
> But there's no misunderstanding how you act and how you live.

Who has been a spiritual mentor to you? _____

3. Facilitate opportunities for others to give.

One Sunday, my family took three children from the church to lunch to celebrate their birthdays. After lunch they planned to spend the afternoon at my house, and then we would return to church for the evening activities.

The day before, one of our church members was admitted to the hospital to have some tests run. After lunch, I asked the children if they would like to accompany me to the hospital to make a ministerial visit. Not knowing exactly what that would involve, they were a little reticent but agreed to go. On the way to the hospital we stopped at a grocery store to buy a card and flowers. When we got back in the car I gave them a quick lesson on hospital etiquette and told them how our visit could minister encouragement and grace to the one who was ill. We decided that one of the children would present the flowers, another would give the card, and one would pray.

It was, of course, a wonderful visit. In some small way, I hope I spurred these three children on toward love and good deeds by serving as a facilitator. I recognized a need, provided transportation, bought the card and flowers, gave a few suggestions, and then stood back and let them do a good deed. I served as a facilitator as they ministered several of the One Anothers—comfort, encourage, pray for, be kind to, prefer, and greet.

Write about the last time you helped facilitate others in the giving of the One Anothers.

_____

_____

4. Affirm others when they give.

Often, we develop a "watchdog" mentality toward those we're around. We watch them closely, try to catch them doing something wrong, and then quickly correct and/or punish them.

But positive reinforcement is always more effective than negative input. Catch people doing something *right*, acknowledge and affirm them, and they will be motivated to do more of the same. So a good way to "spur one another on toward love and good deeds" is to observe people's lives, and when they engage in genuine love, brag on them.

One day, at my office, I was blessed to spend some time with Nicole (age seven) and Faith (age four), while their mothers were in a meeting. While I worked at my desk, they colored pictures and played office. When they were about to leave, I told them I had a present for them. I keep a good inventory of inexpensive gifts in my office closet for times such as this, so I reached in and pulled out a few zippered, clear vinyl bags I had purchased at Office Depot. There was a small bag inside a medium sized bag, inside a large bag. Hmm…three bags, two girls.

Lacking the wisdom of Solomon, I decided to offer the small and medium bags to one of the girls and the large bag to the other. Problem was, I could tell they both wanted the large bag.

First, I asked Faith, the younger child, which bag she wanted, With the most convincing argument she could muster up, she replied, "I have a lot of crayons at home; I *really* think I need the big bag."

I then asked Nicole which gift she preferred. She glanced over at Faith and, seeing the anticipation and desire on her countenance, hesitated for a moment and then replied, "I want the two smaller bags." She *preferred* Faith.

I would suggest that that was a significant, life-shaping moment in Nicole's life. In the moment of hesitation she struggled with selfishness but victoriously yielded to the life-giving power of Romans 12:10: "Prefer one another."

Catch people doing something *right*, acknowledge and affirm them, and they will be motivated to do **more of the same.**

What did I do? I *affirmed* her act of love and her good deed. In private, I told Nicole how proud I was of her and that there is a Bible verse for what she did—"Prefer one another." Perhaps it was the first time she had ever heard the verse. I also bragged on her in front of her mother; Nicole really enjoyed that. Hopefully, I "spurred her on toward love and good deeds" by affirming her.

In general, are you an affirming person? _____

Write about the last time you "caught" someone doing something right and then you praised him or her.

_____

_____

5. Teach others about giving.

There are some aspects of the Christian life that are—let's be honest—ethereal, mystical, and hard to explain. For instance, the fact that the Holy Spirit dwells within us is difficult to explain and, at times, hard to experience. But not so with the One Anothers. They are all action verbs—acts that you do. As such, they can be easily taught. So one way to "spur one another on toward love and good deeds" is simply to teach the One Anothers.

Several years ago I was called to a local church to serve on the pastoral staff. I met a young father one morning in the hallway and he introduced me to his two preschool sons. He said, "Boys, this is pastor Don. Look him in the eye, stand tall, shake his hand, and tell him your name." He was teaching his sons how to Greet One Another.

> Though the One Anothers are basically easy to perform, we should not assume that everyone knows how to do them.

In contrast, I once walked up to a family who was visiting our church and extended my hand of greeting to the daughter who was about eight years old. She just sat there dumbfounded. She didn't know what to do, didn't know to shake my hand, how to receive my greeting, or to smile. The encounter was quite awkward. Obviously, in the first family, the parents were teaching their children how to Greet One Another. In the second family, this was being neglected.

Though the One Anothers are basically easy to perform, we should not assume that everyone knows how to do them. Comfort One Another is really quite simple, but I didn't understand how to do it until I was middle-aged. I thought I was doing quite well at Accept One Another until the Spirit convicted me, after twenty-plus years of marriage, that I was not accepting my *wife* as I should.

That's why I'm convinced that all thirty-five of the One Anothers need to be taught to the body of Christ. Let's *not* assume that everyone knows how to Greet, Confess Sins, Show Hospitality, etc. Let's *teach* them how.

How *Not to* Spur Others On

Often, in order to solidify and clarify an issue, it's helpful to consider its opposite. Polarize the two extremes and they become more obvious. Applied to Hebrews 10:24, the question would be, "Let us consider how we can discourage [stymie, dissuade] others toward love and good deeds." I can think of several ways:

- Preach what to do but don't model—*Do as I say, not as I do.*
- Adopt a "policeman" mentality—*I'm going to watch your life and observe how you perform. I'm keeping a record; you better do right.*
- Motivate by making people feel guilty—*You call yourself a Christian? I need to see more good deeds.*
- Pressure people into a works mentality—*The more good deeds you do, the better off you are and the more pleasing you are to God.*
- Encourage a self-serving attitude—*You need to look out for yourself. If you don't, no one else will.*

Write down the names of five of your close relatives or friends. Then rank them (1 being, "needs improvement" and 10 being, "does a great job") relative to how well they minister the five One Anothers listed below. Then, consider how you can spur each person on toward love and good deeds in the areas that he or she is weak in.

Name	Prefer	Greet	Comfort	Wait for	Confess Sins
_____	____	____	____	____	____
_____	____	____	____	____	____
_____	____	____	____	____	____
_____	____	____	____	____	____
_____	____	____	____	____	____

The *Christian Herald* once carried an article about a senior executive of one of the largest banks in New York City. He told how he had risen to a place of prominence and influence. At first he served as office boy. Then one day the president of the company called him aside and said, "I want you to come into my office and be with me each day." The young man replied, "But what could I do to help you, sir? I don't know anything about finances."

"Never mind that! You will learn what I want to teach you a lot faster if you just *stay by my side* and keep your eyes and ears open!" "That was the most significant experience of my life," said the now-famous banker. "Being with that wise man made me just like him. I began to do things the way he did, and that accounts for what I am today."

Hopefully, at the end of my life there will be many people who will testify that by my giving, modeling, facilitating, affirming, and teaching, I "spurred them on toward love and good deeds."

Personal Journal

1. In your life, who has done the best job of "spurring you on toward love and good deeds"?

_____

2. If you have children, do you see Hebrews 10:24 as part of your parental job description (see Ephesians 6:4)? If so, write out a practical plan for sharing all thirty-five One Anothers with each child.

_____

_____

3. If you are married, do you see Hebrews 10:24 as part of your "job description" as a spouse? If so, write out a practical plan for encouraging your spouse in all thirty-five areas.

_____

_____

4. Write your own definition of Spur One Another on Toward Love and Good Deeds.

_____

_____

5. On a scale from 1 to 10 (1 being, "I need to improve" and 10 being, "I do a good job"), how well do you do at spurring others on toward love and good deeds?

     I rate myself a _____.

Group Time

Each member of the group should give his or her individual response to the first two questions. Allow about two minutes for each person's response. Allow all group members to share answers to question #1 before proceeding to question #2.

1. What was the most interesting concept in this chapter?
2. Share your responses to the first three Personal Journal questions.

As a group, process these discussion questions. The discussion questions have been prioritized. Depending on the time allotted for your group discussion, you may not be able to discuss all the questions.

a. As a group, spend some time considering how to "spur one another on toward love and good deeds." There are five ways mentioned in this chapter—can you think of other ways?
b. How does Hebrews 10:24 relate to the Great Commission (Matthew 28:19–20), particularly the phrase "teaching them to obey all things I have commanded you"?
c. Read 1 Corinthians 11:1; Philippians 3:17; 2 Thessalonians 3:7; and Titus 2:7. What was one of Paul's educational strategies?
d. This chapter presented five ways to "spur one another on"—give, model, facilitate, affirm, and teach. Why is it best to do the first four prior to teaching?
e. Why is Hebrews 10:24 particularly appealing to cowboys? (Just kidding.)